Fun Stops
Colorado

101 Fun Things to Do and Places to See

William C. Herow • Brianna Cattelino

Published by:
Roundabout Publications
PO Box 19235
Lenexa, KS 66285

800-455-2207

www.RoundaboutPublications.com

Contents

Introduction

Fun Stops Colorado offers a wide variety of places to see and fun things to do throughout the state. This easy-to-use guide is divided into three sections as follows:

- Cities and towns with a Fun Stop are shown on a state map. If more than one Fun Stop is located in any city, the number of Fun Stops is listed after the city's name.

- A Quick Reference Chart, arranged alphabetically by city name, provides an overview of each Fun Stop. Included are icons representing the Subject Category (see below), fees that may be charged, and a brief description of each Fun Stop.

- Detailed information about each Fun Stop follows the Quick Reference Chart and is listed alphabetically by name. This section includes each Fun Stop's address, web site, phone number, GPS coordinates, description, operating season and hours, along with driving directions. Also included is the Fun Stop's Subject Category and Subcategory (see below), fees charged, Interstate access, and available facilities.

Refer to the samples on the next page for an explanation of the charts and icons used in this guide.

SUBJECT CATEGORIES

To assist you in finding Fun Stops that interest you, four Subject Categories have been established which represent the different types of Fun Stops. These four categories are included in the Quick Reference Chart. In the detailed information for each Fun Stop, a Subcategory is included to further classify each Subject Category. The following is a list of these Subject Categories and their Subcategories.

Attraction	**Museum**	**Nature & Wildlife**	**Outdoors**
Amusement / Theme Park	Animals & Nature	Arboretum / Garden	Beaches & Coasts
Archaeological Site	Art / Art Gallery	Aquarium / Fish Hatchery	Forests & Wilderness Areas
Cable, Cog, Incline, Train Rides	Aviation	Nature Center	Natural / Scenic Area
	Children's	Petting Zoo / Farm	Park / Recreation Area
Cave	Dolls & Toys	Wildlife Park / Sanctuary	
Cemetery	Estate / Mansion	Wildlife Refuge	
Company / Factory Tour	History - Local	Zoo	
Educational	History - National		
Historic Site	Military		
Memorial / Monument	Music		
Mosaics, Murals & Statues	Railroad / Trains		
Observatory / Planetarium	Religious		
Religious Site	Science		
Restored Settlement / Village	Sports		
Water Park	Vehicles		
Wineries			

QUICK REFERENCE CHART

Below is a sample of the *Quick Reference Chart* identifying the Subject Category icons and the information included in the chart.

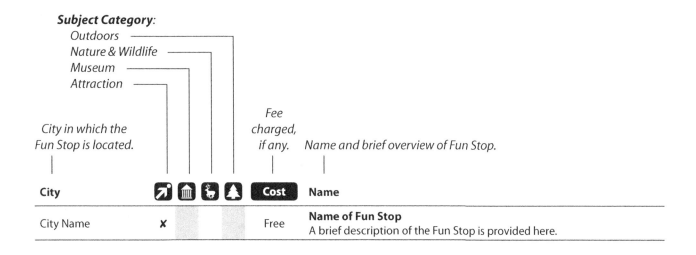

FUN STOP DETAILS

Below is a sample of the detailed information provided for each Fun Stop.

Fun Stop Name
Address

WEB SITE: www.roundaboutpublications.com
PHONE: 800-455-2207
COORDINATES: 38.9686 | -94.7286

DESCRIPTION: Detailed description of Fun Stop. **SEASON & HOURS**: Operating season and hours. **DIRECTIONS**: Directions to the Fun Stop are given here. If a Fun Stop is located within 50 miles of an Interstate highway, directions are given from the exit. Directions for Fun Stops not within 50 miles of an Interstate highway are given from the town's center.

Category
 Subcategory
Fee: Cost, if any.
Interstate:
 Interstate exit and miles
 from highway to fun stop.
Facilities:
 Visitor Center
 Gift Shop
 Picnic Area
 Food
 Camping
 Lodging

Please Note: The information in this sidebar changes depending on a Fun Stop's distance from an Interstate highway and the availability of facilites. For example, if a Fun Stop is greater than 50 miles from an Interstate highway, the Interstate information is omitted. Likewise, only the facilities available at a Fun Stop are listed. If a Fun Stop does not offer any of the facilities, the entire Facilities section is omitted.

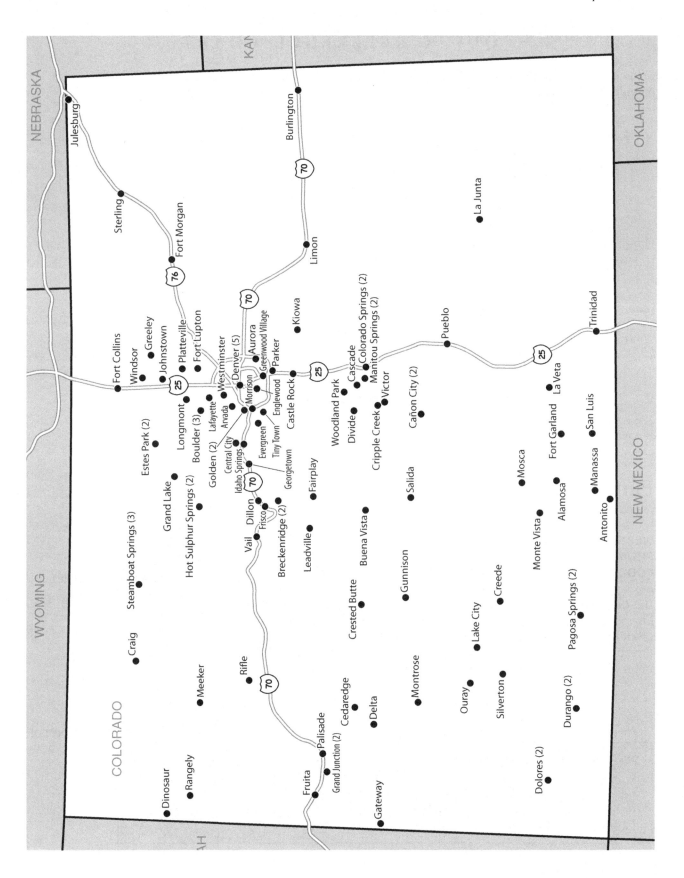

City	⬈	🏛	🦌	🌲	Cost	Name
Alamosa			X		Free	**Alamosa National Wildlife Refuge** — Wildlife refuge in the San Luis Valley. Fishing, hunting, and wildlife observation are among the activities available.
Antonito	X				$75.00+	**Cumbres & Toltec Scenic Railroad** — America's highest and longest narrow gauge scenic railroad.
Arvada		X			$7.00	**Cussler Museum** — A collection of rare and vintage automobiles from all over the world.
Aurora				X	Free	**Plains Conservation Center** — An outdoor education facility and state-designated natural area.
Boulder	X				Free	**Celestial Seasonings** — See how Celestial Seasonings tea is blended, packaged, and shipped.
		X			Free	**Leanin' Tree Museum and Sculpture Garden of Western Art** — Features fine art paintings and bronzes of western America created after 1930.
		X			$5.00	**Shelby American Collection** — Museum dedicated to the history and preservation of Shelby American automobiles.
Breckenridge	X				$19.00	**Country Boy Mine** — Tours of an historic and restored gold mining site.
		X			$5.00	**Red, White & Blue Fire Museum** — History of the Breckenridge Fire Department.
Buena Vista		X			$5.00	**Buena Vista Heritage Museum** — Displays and information about the history of Buena Vista and Chaffee County.
Burlington		X			$6.00	**Old Town Museum** — Restored buildings and artifacts from the turn-of-the-century.
Cañon City	X				$20.00	**Buckskin Joe Frontier Town and Railway** — Recreated old west town and scenic train ride with views of the Royal Gorge.
		X			$7.00	**Museum of Colorado Prisons** — Presents the history of the Colorado Prison System through exhibits that trace the prison life of Colorado's most infamous criminals.
Cascade	X				$17.95	**Santa's Workshop/North Pole** — A Christmas themed family amusement park.
Castle Rock		X			Free	**Castle Rock Museum** — Preserves the local history and heritage in a fun and educational manner.
Cedaredge	X				$3.00	**Pioneer Town Museum** — Restored buildings and authentic artifacts depicting pioneer life in Colorado.
Central City		X			$5.00	**The Gilpin History Museum** — On display are several collections and artifacts showing what was popular in the town of Gilpin during its most thriving period.
Colorado Springs		X			Free	**Pikes Peak Radio & Electronics Museum** — Explains the history of the radio and other electronics and honors the men most important in developing those technologies.

City	⬈	🏛	🦌	🌲	Cost	Name
	x				$6.00	**Rock Ledge Ranch Historic Site** A living history farm and museum depicting life in the Pikes Peak region from the late 1700's to the early 1900's.
Craig		x			Free	**Museum of Northwest Colorado** Overview of the history of Northwestern Colorado through displays of cowboy and railroad artifacts and old photographs of the region.
Creede		x			$7.00	**Creede Underground Mining Museum** Explores the mining history of Creede, Colorado. All facilities are underground.
Crested Butte		x			$3.00	**Mountain Bike Hall of Fame** Commemorates the development of the sport of mountain biking and the individuals who made significant contributions.
Cripple Creek	x				$15.00	**Mollie Kathleen Gold Mine** Tours of America's only vertical shaft gold mine.
Delta		x			$4.00	**Fort Uncompahgre History Museum** Museum consisting of seven re-created cabins on the banks of the Gunnison River.
Denver	x				Free	**Colorado State Capitol** Historical and Legislative tours of the Colorado State Capitol building.
		x			$6.00	**Denver Firefighters Museum** History of firefighting and the Denver Fire Department.
		x			$6.00	**Denver Museum of Miniatures, Dolls and Toys** Museum displaying fully furnished miniature houses, trains, planes, cars, antique dolls, and a miniature circus.
		x			$11.00	**Denver Museum of Nature & Science** Collection of artifacts relating to all areas of the sciences.
	x				Free	**United States Mint** Guided tours of the United States Mint at Denver.
Dillon		x			$6.00	**Dillon Schoolhouse Museum** Gives visitors the opportunity to experience the feel of an authentic school day in Dillon's past.
Dinosaur			x		Free	**Dinosaur National Monument** Public land area managed by the National Park Service featuring dinosaur fossils, petroglyphs, pictographs, and more.
Divide			x		$10.00	**Colorado Wolf & Wildlife Center** Guided educational tours that focus on dispelling myths about wolves.
Dolores	x				Free	**Canyons of the Ancients National Monument** Bureau of Land Management area containing a large number of archaeological sites representing Ancestral Puebloan and other Native American cultures.
		x			Free	**Galloping Goose Historical Society** The restored Dolores Depot serves as a museum with artifacts from the original Rio Grande Southern Railroad.
Durango		x			Call	**Discovery Museum at the Powerhouse** An interactive museum designed to teach visitors about different power technologies.
	x				$81.00+	**Durango & Silverton Narrow Gauge Railroad & Museum** A narrow-gauge scenic train ride through the San Juan Mountains.

City	🏃	🏛	🦌	🌲	Cost	Name
Englewood		✗			Free	**Museum of Outdoor Arts** A variety of exhibits are displayed year-round at the museum's headquarters in addition to permanent outdoor displays throughout the city.
Estes Park		✗			$3.00	**MacGregor Ranch and Museum** A working cattle ranch, museum, and educational center.
		✗			Free	**Stanley Museum of Estes Park** Celebrates the significance of the Stanley Steamer automobile and explores the history of the family responsible for it.
Evergreen		✗			Free	**Hiwan Homestead Museum** The restored summer home of Colorado's aristocratic society which is now used as a museum to show the mountain life-style of the early 20th century.
Fairplay		✗			$8.00	**South Park City Museum** South Park City is a museum of over forty restored buildings designed to represent what a Colorado mining boomtown would be like.
Fort Collins		✗			$7.00	**Bee Family Centennial Farm** The museum educates visitors about the history of agriculture in Northern Colorado through the personal lives of the Bee family farmers and several interactive exhibits and activites.
Fort Garland		✗			$5.00	**Fort Garland Museum** A recreation of Fort Garland as it was under the command of frontiersman Kit Carson. Nearby is the reconstructed campsite of Zebulon Pike and his men during the winter of 1806-1807.
Fort Lupton		✗			$5.00	**Fort Lupton Museum** Explores the history and traditions of the families who have lived in and around Fort Lupton since the mid 1800's through continuously changing exhibits.
Fort Morgan		✗			Free	**Fort Morgan Museum** The past is preserved in the Fort Morgan Museum through a number of exhibits exploring the people, stories, and artifacts of Fort Morgan.
Frisco		✗			Free	**Frisco Historic Park and Museum** The park and museum consists of several buildings all displaying a different part of Frisco's history.
Fruita		✗			$7.00	**Dinosaur Journey Museum** An interactive museum which investigates the history of dinosaurs in Colorado.
Gateway		✗			$9.00	**The Gateway Colorado Auto Museum** A showing of the history, science, design and social impact of the American car.
Georgetown		✗			Free	**Georgetown Energy Museum** Shows the evolution of electricity as it gained popularity through the inventions of machines which used the power.
Golden		✗			$5.00	**Buffalo Bill Museum and Grave** A tribute to the life of William F. "Buffalo Bill" Cody set at the site of his burial on Lookout Mountain.
	✗				Free	**National Renewable Energy Laboratory Visitors Center** Self-guided tours through an interactive exhibit featuring information about renewable energy sources.

City	🡕	🏛	🦌	🌲	Cost	Name
Grand Junction		✗			$4.00	**Cross Orchards Historic Farm** A museum containing a wide variety of household items, farming and construction tools of the west, and a railway exhibit.
		✗			$5.50	**Museum of Western Colorado** Museum representing a thousand years of history.
Grand Lake		✗			$3.00	**Kauffman House Museum** An example of a late 19th century hotel and a museum housing artifacts from the local people of the past.
Greeley		✗			Free	**Greeley History Museum** The museum displays both the important and anonymous figures in Greeley's past through a number of permanent and changing exhibits.
Greenwood Village		✗			Free	**The Madden Museum of Art** Features an extensive gallery from the personal collection of a local businessman and his wife.
Gunnison		✗			$7.00	**Gunnison Pioneer & Train Museum** The museum's collection represents the early heritage of Gunnison County.
Hot Sulphur Springs		✗			$5.00	**Cozens Ranch & Stage Stop Museum 1874** The original home of William Zane Cozens who established the post office and ran the stage stop in Fraser Valley.
		✗			$5.00	**Pioneer Village Museum** Teaches visitors about the history and struggles of the early pioneers in Colorado.
Idaho Springs		✗			Free	**James Underhill Museum** The early 20th century home of James Underhill, a prominent Colorado surveyor and mining engineer.
Johnstown		✗			Free	**Johnstown Parish House Museum** The Parish House combines exhibits displaying its local history with those presenting the broader history of agriculture and the expansion west.
Julesburg		✗			$1.00	**Fort Sedgwick Museum** Features exhibits diplaying the history of Fort Sedgwick, the town of Julesburg, and northeastern Colorado.
Kiowa		✗			Free	**Elbert County Historical Society and Museum** A museum dedicated to preserving and presenting the history of Elbert County from prehistoric times through the turn-of-the-century.
La Junta	✗				$3.00	**Bent's Old Fort National Historic Site** Reconstructed 1840's adobe fur trading post.
La Veta		✗			Free	**Francisco Fort Museum** An old adobe fort, schoolhouse, saloon, and blacksmith displaying photographs and other items related to the history of the West.
Lafayette		✗			Free	**Lafayette Miners Museum** At one time the home of miners, the museum focuses on the history of Lafayette with an emphasis on mining.
Lake City	✗				$10.00	**Hard Tack Mine** Silver mine tour and museum.
Leadville		✗			$7.00	**The National Mining Hall of Fame & Museum** History of mining through hands-on exhibits. The Hall of Fame honors those most important in the development of mining techniques.

City	↗	🏛	🦌	🌲	Cost	Name
Limon		X			Free	**Limon Heritage Museum** Depicts the different aspects of a life on the plains.
Longmont		X			Free	**Saint Stephen's Church** Church built in 1881 as the first home for the congregation of Saint Stephen's Episcopal parish.
Manassa		X			Free	**The Jack Dempsey Museum** A museum commemorating the life and achievements of heavyweight boxer, and Manassa native, Jack Dempsey.
Manitou Springs	X				$8.00	**Miramont Castle** 14,000 square foot mansion with over 40 rooms built in nine different architectural styles including several eight-sided rooms.
	X				$33.00	**Pikes Peak Cog Railway** Train ride to the top of Pikes Peak.
Meeker		X			Free	**White River Museum** Contains the personal effects of the town's namesake, Nathan C. Meeker, his family, men and women important to the history of Meeker, and several artifacts that once belonged to the Ute Indians.
Monte Vista			X		Free	**Monte Vista National Wildlife Refuge** Wildlife refuge in the San Luis Valley. Fishing, hunting, and wildlife observation are among the activities available.
Montrose		X			$4.00	**Ute Indian Museum** A tribute to Chief Ouray and the Ute Indians, the museum houses one of the most complete collections of Ute artifacts.
Morrison	X				Free	**Dinosaur Ridge** Visitor center and interpretive trails explain the local geology, dinosaur fossils, and more.
Mosca			X		$15.00	**Colorado Gators** Reptile refuge containing over 300 alligators and other wildlife.
Ouray	X				$16.95	**Bachelor-Syracuse Mine** Guided tour of a silver and gold mine.
Pagosa Springs	X				$10.00	**Chimney Rock Archaeological Area** Archaeological site that was home to the ancestors of the modern Pueblo Indians 1,000 years ago.
		X			$4.00	**Fred Harman Art Museum** A presentation of the western art created by Fred Harman. Additionally, exhibits dedicated to the history of the Red Ryder comic strip produced by Harman are on display.
Palisade	X				Free	**Grande River Vineyards** Winery and vineyard tours.
Parker		X			$10.00	**The Wildlife Experience** An educational and entertaining museum about the world's wildlife and ecosystems.
Platteville		X			$1.00	**Fort Vasquez Museum** Follows the path of founders Louis Vasquez and Andrew Sublette and allows visitors a glimpse at the fur trading past.
Pueblo		X			Free	**InfoZone News Museum** The museum illustrates the history of the newspaper in Colorado as well as across the United States.

City	⬈	🏛	🦌	🌲	Cost	Name
Rangely		X			Free	**Rangely Museum Society** Presentation of Rangely's past through the oral testaments of its senior citizens, old photographs, and other historical exhibits.
Rifle				X	$6.00	**Rifle Falls State Park** State park featuring a scenic triple waterfall. A variety of outdoor activities are available including biking, camping, fishing, hiking, hunting, picnicking, cross-country skiing, and snowmobiling.
Salida		X			$3.00	**Salida Museum** Houses artifacts that display the culture-rich past of Salida, Colorado.
San Luis	X				Free	**Shrine of the Stations of the Cross** Shrine featuring life-size sculptures depicting the last hours of Christ's life.
Silverton	X				$16.95	**Old Hundred Gold Mine Tour** Guided gold mine tours.
Steamboat Springs	X				$10.00	**Strawberry Park Natural Hot Springs** Features 104-degree mineral water pools, massage huts, and Watsu therapy.
		X			$5.00	**Tread of Pioneers Museum** Traces the agricultural and cultural past of Routt County, exploring several different avenues of history along the way.
			X		Free	**Yampa River Botanic Park** High altitude park containing a variety of plants, trees, and shrubs.
Sterling		X			$3.00	**Overland Trail Museum** Named after the Overland trail stage route, the museum and other restored buildings on the site outline historic, westward expansion of pioneers.
Tiny Town	X				$5.00	**Tiny Town and Railroad** Over 100 colorful, kid-sized buildings constructed at the former site of the Denver-Leadville stagecoach stop. Also features train rides through the village.
Trinidad		X			$3.00	**Arthur Roy Mitchell Museum** A museum featuring the western art of Arthur Roy Mitchell and other artists.
Vail		X			Free	**Colorado Ski & Snowboard Museum and Hall of Fame** Honors indivduals who have made contributions to the sport of skiing in Colorado in addition to the history of skiing and snowboarding.
Victor		X			$4.00	**Lowell Thomas Museum** Tells the story of the gold rush in Victor, Colorado and celebrates the life of Lowell Thomas, a Victor native, famous journalist, and world traveler.
Westminster			X		$8.50	**Butterfly Pavilion and Insect Center** Interactive exhibits teach visitors about invertebrates and conservation.
Windsor		X			Free	**Windsor Museum** Displays Windsor, Colorado, from a historical perspective as visitors travel through the reconstructed buildings important to the town at the turn-of-the-century.
Woodland Park		X			$11.50	**Rocky Mountain Dinosaur Resource Center** A family-friendly museum containing collections of dinosaur fossils, skeletons, and interactive learning exhibits.

Alamosa National Wildlife Refuge
9383 El Rancho Ln, Alamosa CO 81101

WEB SITE: www.fws.gov/alamosa
PHONE: 719-589-4021
COORDINATES: 37.4393 | -105.8028

Nature & Wildlife
Wildlife Refuge
Fee: Free
Facilities:
Visitor Center

DESCRIPTION: Alamosa National Wildlife Refuge is located in the heart of Colorado's San Luis Valley. The refuge contains over 11,000 acres of wetlands and supports a variety of wildlife including songbirds, water birds, raptors, mule deer, beaver, and coyotes. Recreational activities include fishing, hunting, photography, and wildlife observation. The refuge also offers self-guided auto and walking tours. **SEASON & HOURS**: Daylight hours, year-round; visitor center open 7:30am to 4pm, Monday thru Friday except Federal holidays. **DIRECTIONS**: From Alamosa go east 4 miles on US-160 then south 2 miles on El Rancho Ln.

Arthur Roy Mitchell Museum
150 E Main St, Trinidad CO 81082

WEB SITE: www.armitchell.org
PHONE: 719-846-4224
COORDINATES: 37.1688 | -104.5046

Museum
Art/Art Gallery
Fee: $3
Interstate:
I-25 Exit 13B; .5 mile
Facilities:
Gift Shop
Picnic Area

DESCRIPTION: The A.R. Mitchell Museum houses 350 paintings by Mitchell as well as paintings created by other artists of his time such as Harvey Dunn, Harold Von Schmidt, Nick Eggenhoffer, Larry Heller, Grant Reynard and Ned Jacob. A collection of Spanish folk art is also on display, including an elk painting believed to be created by a Franciscan monk from the early 1700's. A number of historic photographs taken by Trinidad natives spanning over 100 years are also exhibited. **SEASON & HOURS**: May through October, Tuesday through Saurday, 10am to 4pm; Sunday, Noon to 4pm. **DIRECTIONS**: From I-25 Exit 13B go east .5 mile on Main St/US-160.

Bachelor-Syracuse Mine
1222 CR 14, Ouray CO 81427

WEB SITE: www.bachelorsyracusemine.com
PHONE: 970-325-0220 or 888-227-4585
COORDINATES: 38.0596 | -107.6786

Attraction
Historic Site
Fee: $16.95
Facilities:
Gift Shop
Food

DESCRIPTION: Visitors are taken 1,800 feet horizontally into Gold Hill, rich in gold, silver, and other precious metals. Guests are accompanied by a trained guide who has first-hand experience working the mine. Visitors will see the equipment used in mining, the rich silver veins and other mineral deposits. The stopes, declines, crosscuts, run-a-rounds and drifts are explained to guests. Visitors will also see the work areas and learn how explosives are used in the mining process. Tours are about one hour in length. **SEASON & HOURS**: Late May to mid-September; daily, 9am to 5pm (4pm spring and fall). **DIRECTIONS**: From Ouray, go north 2 miles on US-550 then east 1.2 miles on CR-14.

Bee Family Centennial Farm
4320 E County Road 58, Fort Collins CO 80524

WEB SITE: www.beefamilyfarm.com
PHONE: 970-482-9168
COORDINATES: 40.6680 | -104.9960

Museum
Animals & Nature
Fee: $7
Interstate:
I-25 Exit 271; 4.5 miles or
I-25 Exit 278; 2.8 miles
Facilities:
Gift Shop

DESCRIPTION: The museum was created from what was once a 160-acre farm and homestead and remains, to this day, a working family farm. On display in the museum are wide assortments of artifacts including farming equipment, cars, wagons, living necessities, letters, diaries, and pictures, several of which date back to 1894. On site are several animals, which visitors can see as they tour the farm. A scavenger hunt is offered as well as a number of other interactive activities that teach children about the daily chores on a farm. **SEASON & HOURS**: May through October, Fridays and Saturdays, 9am to 4pm. **DIRECTIONS**: Northbound I-25 travelers should use Exit 271 then go east to the frontage road; go north 4.1 miles to CR-58 then go east .2 mile. Southbound travelers should use Exit 278 then go east to the frontage road; go south 2.5 miles to CR-58 then go east .2 mile.

Bent's Old Fort National Historic Site
35110 SH 194, La Junta CO 81050

WEB SITE: www.nps.gov/beol/
PHONE: 719-383-5010
COORDINATES: 38.0439 | -103.4317

Attraction
Historic Site
Fee: $3
Facilities:
Gift Shop

DESCRIPTION: Bent's Old Fort is a reconstructed 1840's adobe fur trading post on the mountain branch of the Santa Fe Trail where traders, trappers, travelers, and Plains Indian tribes came together for trade. Living history interpreters in period clothing recreate the past with guided tours, demonstrations, and special events. Visitors can also explore the fort on their own using a self-guided tour booklet. Living history demonstrations occur June through September. Guided tours available September through May. **SEASON & HOURS**: Year-round, daily, 8am to 5:30pm in summer and 9am to 4pm the rest of the year. **DIRECTIONS**: From La Junta, go north .8 mile on SR-109 then east 6.4 miles on SR-194.

Buckskin Joe Frontier Town and Railway
1193 Fremont County Road 3A, Canon City CO 81212

WEB SITE: www.buckskinjoe.com
PHONE: 719-275-5149 or 719-275-5485
COORDINATES: 38.4780 | -105.3285

Attraction
Restored Settlement / Village
Fee: $20
Interstate:
I-25 Exit 101; 45.3 miles.
Facilities:
Gift Shop

DESCRIPTION: Buckskin Joe Frontier Town is modeled after an original mining town near Alma, Colorado. Established in 1958, the recreated old west town has been the site of over 21 feature films. Authentic buildings and gunfights provide entertainment for visitors. The attraction also offers a 3-mile, 30-minute train ride over wooden trestles to view the Royal Gorge. **SEASON & HOURS**: Open daily mid-June to mid-August, 9:30am to 6pm. **DIRECTIONS**: From I-25 Exit 101 go west 44 miles on US-50 then south 1.3 miles on CR-3A.

Buena Vista Heritage Museum

506 E Main St, Buena Vista CO 81211

WEB SITE: http://buenavistaheritage.org/Page.aspx?PageID=2355
PHONE: 719-395-8458
COORDINATES: 38.8433 | -106.1273

Museum
History - Local
Fee: $5
Facilities:
Gift Shop

DESCRIPTION: The old Chaffee County Courthouse, completed in 1882, now houses the Buena Vista Heritage Museum. Various rooms display numerous artifacts from the 1880's. The Fashions Room contains many interesting clothing items including several wedding dresses, petticoats, undergarments, hats, shoes, etc. A collection of rocks, minerals, and semiprecious gemstones are on display in the Commerce and Industry Room. The Schoolroom has many pictures of Buena Vista's graduating classes and annuals. A resource room is available to anyone researching local history. **SEASON & HOURS**: Memorial Day Weekend through September, Monday through Saturday, 10am to 5pm; Sunday, Noon to 5pm. **DIRECTIONS**: In town, 3 blocks east of US-24 on Main St.

Buffalo Bill Museum and Grave

987½ Lookout Mountain Rd, Golden CO 80401

WEB SITE: www.buffalobill.org
PHONE: 303-526-0744
COORDINATES: 39.7318 | -105.2396

Museum
History - National
Fee: $5
Interstate:
I-70 Exit 256; 4.2 miles
Facilities:
Visitor Center
Gift Shop
Food

DESCRIPTION: Set at the site of Buffalo Bill's grave, the museum has a number of permanent exhibits that trace Bill's life before and during his career as a traveling entertainer as well as exhibits displaying Indian artifacts, Western art and firearms. Special events include a celebration of Buffalo Bill's birthday every February. **SEASON & HOURS**: May through October, daily, 9am to 5pm; November through April 30, daily, 9am to 4pm. **DIRECTIONS**: From I-70 Exit 256 follow US-40 west 1.4 miles, turn right on Lookout Mountain Rd and follow for 2.8 miles.

Butterfly Pavilion and Insect Center

6252 W 104th Ave, Westminster CO 80020

WEB SITE: www.butterflies.org
PHONE: 303-469-5441
COORDINATES: 39.8864 | -105.0675

Nature & Wildlife
Zoo
Fee: $8.50
Interstate:
I-25 Exit 221; 4.4 miles
Facilities:
Gift Shop
Food

DESCRIPTION: The Butterfly Pavilion combines science education with interactive fun to teach visitors about invertebrates and conservation. Five immersive exhibits are featured, including a rainforest filled with 1,200 free-flying tropical butterflies. Visitors can get up close and personal with live animals, enjoy daily educational programs, or explore the outdoors on the nature trail. **SEASON & HOURS**: Open daily year-round, 9am to 5pm. **DIRECTIONS**: From I-25 Exit 221 go west 4.3 miles on 104th Ave then south .1 mile on Westminster Blvd.

Canyons of the Ancients National Monument

27501 Highway 184, Dolores CO 81323

WEB SITE: www.blm.gov/co/st/en/nm/canm.html
PHONE: 970-882-5600
COORDINATES: 37.4750 | -108.5471

DESCRIPTION: Canyons of the Ancients National Monument in southwestern Colorado contains a huge number of archaeological sites—more than 6,000 recorded so far—representing Ancestral Puebloan and other Native American cultures. Visitors planning to explore the Monument should first stop at the Anasazi Heritage Center for maps, information, and current conditions. Numerous artifacts from excavations within the Monument are housed at the Heritage Center. Lowry Pueblo National Historic Landmark is the only developed recreation site within the Monument. The Pueblo has standing walls that have been stabilized, 40 rooms, eight kivas, and a Great Kiva. The site has a handicapped accessible picnic area, toilet, and trail. There is no water or phone service. Primitive camping is permitted throughout the Monument except at Lowry Pueblo. **SEASON & HOURS**: Open year-round. **DIRECTIONS**: From Cortez, go east 2 miles on US-160 then north 7.8 miles on SR-145; turn left at SR-184 and follow 1.2 miles to visitor center.

Attraction
Archaeological Site
Fee: Free
Facilities:
Visitor Center
Picnic Area
Camping

Castle Rock Museum

420 Elbert St, Castle Rock CO 80104

WEB SITE: www.castlerockmuseum.org
PHONE: 303-814-3164
COORDINATES: 39.3740 | -104.8625

DESCRIPTION: The museum is located in the Denver & Rio Grande Railroad Depot, constructed in 1874 when Castle Rock was selected as the county seat. Exhibits promote education about the local heritage of Castle Rock and the surrounding areas through numerous photographs and artifacts. Walking tours of downtown Castle Rock are offered the third Saturday of every month from May to October. **SEASON & HOURS**: Year-round, Wednesday through Friday, Noon to 5pm; Saturday, 11am to 4pm. **DIRECTIONS**: From I-25 Exit 182 follow Wilcox St south .5 mile then go west .1 mile on 4th and north on Elbert St.

Museum
History - Local
Fee: Free
Interstate:
I-25 Exit 182; .6 mile

Celestial Seasonings

4600 Sleepytime Dr, Boulder CO 80301

WEB SITE: www.celestialseasonings.com/visit-us/
PHONE: 303-581-1202 or 303-530-5300
COORDINATES: 40.0584 | -105.2190

DESCRIPTION: Free tours of the Celestial Seasonings plant shows you how their tea is blended, packaged, and shipped. Tours leave on the hour and are 45 minutes in length. Free samples of every tea they make is available. Visitors can also browse the extensive display of original artwork that appears on tea boxes. **SEASON & HOURS**: Tours offered daily except on holidays, Monday through Saturday, 10am to 4pm; Sunday, 11am to 4pm. **DIRECTIONS**: From I-25 Exit 235 go west 11 miles on SR-52 then go southwest 1.3 miles on SR-119 to 63rd St; go south on 63rd St .5 mile, southwest 1 mile on Spine Rd and then west .2 mile on Sleepytime Dr.

Attraction
Company/Factory Tour
Fee: Free
Interstate:
I-25 Exit 235; 14 miles
Facilities:
Gift Shop

Chimney Rock Archaeological Area
PO Box 1662, Pagosa Springs CO 81147

WEB SITE: www.chimneyrockco.org/mainnew.htm
PHONE: 970-883-5359 or 970-264-2287
COORDINATES: 37.1897 | -107.3100

Attraction
Archaeological Site
Fee: $10
Facilities:
Visitor Center
Picnic Area

DESCRIPTION: Chimney Rock is a San Juan National Forest Archaeological Area located between Durango and Pagosa Springs. Guided walking tours are offered daily and typically average 2 1/2 hours. Chimney Rock lies on 4,100 acres of national forest land surrounded by the Southern Ute Indian Reservation. The site was home to the ancestors of the modern Pueblo Indians 1,000 years ago and is of great spiritual significance to these tribes. Their ancestors built over 200 homes and ceremonial buildings high above the valley floor, probably to be near the sacred twin rock pinnacles. Since the 1960's, Dr. Frank Eddy of the University of Colorado and others have studied the site, and research continues. **SEASON & HOURS**: Open daily mid-May thru September, 9am to 4:30pm. **DIRECTIONS**: From Pagosa Springs travel 16.5 miles west on US-160 and then south 3 miles on SR-151.

Colorado Gators
9162 Lane 9 N, Mosca CO 81146

WEB SITE: www.gatorfarm.com
PHONE: 719-378-2612
COORDINATES: 37.7058 | -105.8705

Nature & Wildlife
Wildlife Park / Sanctuary
Fee: $15
Facilities:
Gift Shop

DESCRIPTION: Originally started as a fish farm for growing tilapia and African perch, the farm has grown to become a reptile refuge and bird sanctuary. A geothermal well on the property creates ponds and wetlands for the alligators, but also provides a habitat for various waterfowl. The Two Mile Creek Wildlife Habitat lets visitors view alligators, reptiles, and birds in a natural setting. Over 125 species of birds have been seen at the farm. Educational programs aim to teach people about the biology, behavior, and ecological role of reptiles. **SEASON & HOURS**: Open daily year-round. Summer hours are 9am to 7pm; rest of year, 9am to 5pm. **DIRECTIONS**: From Alamosa go north 16 miles on SR-17 then east .4 miles on Ninemile Ln.

Colorado Ski & Snowboard Museum and Hall of Fame
231 S Frontage Rd, Vail CO 81657

WEB SITE: www.skimuseum.net
PHONE: 970-476-1876
COORDINATES: 39.6425 | -106.3727

Museum
Sports
Fee: Free
Interstate:
I-70 Exit 176; .3 mile
Facilities:
Gift Shop

DESCRIPTION: The museum celebrates the history of skiing and snowboarding with its Ski & Snowboard Hall of Fame, tracing the lives of the important men and women who made significant contributions to the advancement of the sports. Included in the museum are collections of skiing artifacts spanning 130 years, a timeline of Colorado skiing, Olympic memorabilia, and the evolution of Snowboarding. **SEASON & HOURS**: Year-round, 10am to 6pm (April and May, 10am to 5pm). **DIRECTIONS**: From I-70 Exit 176 go south of exit 200 feet and then east .3 mile on the frontage road.

Colorado State Capitol
200 E Colfax Ave, Denver CO 80203

WEB SITE: www.colorado.gov
PHONE: 303-866-2167
COORDINATES: 39.7400 | -104.9848

DESCRIPTION: Historical tours of the Colorado State Capitol building include information about early Colorado history, Capitol construction, and the lawmaking process. Visitors will also see several stained glass windows, the Women's Gold Tapestry, and presidential portraits. Tours include a stop outside the Senate and House of Representatives' chambers. Tours are 45 minutes in length. **SEASON & HOURS**: Year-round, summer hours are 9am to 3:30pm; winter hours are 9:15am to 2:30pm. **DIRECTIONS**: From I-25 Exit 210A go east 1.6 miles on Colfax Ave.

Attraction
  Historic Site
Fee: Free
Interstate:
  I-25 Exit 210A; 1.6 miles
Facilities:
  Gift Shop
  Food

Colorado Wolf & Wildlife Center
PO Box 713, Divide CO 80814

WEB SITE: www.wolfeducation.org
PHONE: 719-687-9742
COORDINATES: 38.9305 | -105.2119

DESCRIPTION: The Colorado Wolf & Wildlife Center conducts educational tours and programs that focus on dispelling myths about wolves and wild canids. Tours cover topics such as pack hierarchy, territory, communication, prey impact, and conservation. Visitors will learn about the history of each wolf, coyote, and fox at the Center. Tours last 60 to 75 minutes on average. Reservations are required. **SEASON & HOURS**: Tours are conducted year-round Tuesday through Sunday at 10am, 12pm, and 2pm plus 4pm in the spring/summer season. **DIRECTIONS**: From I-25 Exit 141 go west 26.6 miles on US-24 then south 1.6 miles on CR-42/Twin Rocks Rd.

Nature & Wildlife
  Wildlife Park / Sanctuary
Fee: $10
Interstate:
  I-25 Exit 141; 28.2 miles
Facilities:
  Visitor Center
  Gift Shop

Country Boy Mine
0542 French Gulch Rd, Breckenridge CO 80424

WEB SITE: www.countryboymine.com
PHONE: 970-453-4405
COORDINATES: 39.4822 | -106.0162

DESCRIPTION: Established in 1887, Country Boy Mine was one of the largest and most famous gold mines in Breckenridge. Tours start at the top of every hour and last about 45 minutes. Visitors wear hard hats as they venture 1,000 feet into the mine. Original mining equipment, photos, and other exhibits are on display around the mining site. Visitors can spend some time panning for gold in Eureka Creek. Children enjoy petting the gentle and friendly burros that roam the site. **SEASON & HOURS**: Open mid-May through April. Summer hours: daily, 10am to 4pm; Fall hours: Wednesday through Saturday, 11am to 2pm; Winter hours: Wednesday through Sunday, 11am to 1pm. **DIRECTIONS**: Two miles east of downtown Breckenridge. From town center at Main St

Attraction
  Historic Site
Fee: $19
Interstate:
  I-70 Exit 203; 10 miles
Facilities:
  Gift Shop

and Ski Hill Rd, go north .25 mile and turn right (east) at Wellington Rd. Continue east on Wellington Rd for 1.1 miles. Turn right at French Gulch Rd and follow for .8 mile. Breckenridge is ten miles south of I-70 Exit 203.

Cozens Ranch & Stage Stop Museum 1874
PO Box 165, Hot Sulphur Springs CO 80452

WEB SITE: www.grandcountymuseum.com/CozensRanchM.htm
PHONE: 970-725-3939
COORDINATES: 39.9325 | -105.7909

DESCRIPTION: The museum offers a look at the staging and freighting history of Grand County. In the stage stop adjacent to the home is an authentic replica of an old stagecoach and an explanation of 19th century stagecoach travel. **SEASON & HOURS**: Wednesday through Saturday, 10am to 4pm. **DIRECTIONS**: From I-70 Exit 232 follow US-40 west for approximately 29 miles.

Museum
History - Local
Fee: $5
Interstate:
I-70 Exit 232; 29 miles
Facilities:
Gift Shop

Creede Underground Mining Museum
Forest Service Rd 503 #9, Creede CO 81130

WEB SITE: www.creede.com/mining_museum.htm
PHONE: 719-658-0811
COORDINATES: 37.8577 | -106.9276

DESCRIPTION: The Creede Underground Mining Museum is an authentic example of the techniques used during the process of creating a mine. Inside the museum is much of the equipment used by miners and a mineral display showing the types of rocks that were commonly found while mining. The museum, gift shop, and community center are all underground. **SEASON & HOURS**: Open daily year-round from 10am to 4pm (10am to 3pm weekdays only during winter). **DIRECTIONS**: From town center follow Main St north .7 mile.

Museum
History - Local
Fee: $7
Facilities:
Gift Shop

Cross Orchards Historic Farm
3073 F Road, Grand Junction CO 81504

WEB SITE: www.museumofwesternco.com/visit/cross-orchards-historic-site/
PHONE: 970-434-9814
COORDINATES: 39.0917 | -108.4832

DESCRIPTION: Located on the site of an orchard that once stretched across 243 acres of land, Cross Orchards Historic Farm is the perfect setting to learn about farming equipment, household tools, and the history of the Swanson family's move from Sweden to Cross Orchards. Visitors can also examine the recreated Uintah Railway exhibit and reconstructed depot. Making the visit more realistic are costumed volunteers who guide you along your tour of the farm. **SEASON & HOURS**: April through October, Tuesday through Saturday, 9am to 4pm. **DIRECTIONS**: From I-70 Exit 37 go south .8 mile on I-70-BUS then west 1.6 miles on F Rd.

Museum
History - Local
Fee: $4
Interstate:
I-70 Exit 37; 2.4 miles
Facilities:
Gift Shop

Cumbres & Toltec Scenic Railroad
5234 B Hwy 285, Antonito CO 81120

WEB SITE: www.cumbrestoltec.com
PHONE: 888-286-2737
COORDINATES: 37.0693 | -106.0117

Attraction
Cable, Cog, Incline, Train Rides
Fee: $75 and up
Facilities:
Gift Shop
Picnic Area

DESCRIPTION: The Cumbres & Toltec is a 64-mile scenic train ride between Antonito, Colorado, and Chama, New Mexico. There are 8 trip itineraries but the most common is a round-trip ride to Osier, Colorado, then back to the departure depot. Travelers are given lunch in Osier and one hour to enjoy the mountain scenery. Passengers can choose to ride in one of three types of cars: Coach, Tourist, and Parlor. An open-air observation car is accessible to all passengers. **SEASON & HOURS**: Daily, mid-May to mid-October. **DIRECTIONS**: The Antonito, Colorado, depot is located at the intersection of US-285 and SR-17, on the southern edge of town. Antonito is 30 miles south of Alamosa.

Cussler Museum
14959 W 69th Ave, Arvada CO 80007

WEB SITE: www.cusslermuseum.com
PHONE: 303-420-2795
COORDINATES: 39.8234 | -105.1677

Museum
Vehicles
Fee: $7
Interstate:
I-70 Exit 266; 4.5 miles
Facilities:
Gift Shop

DESCRIPTION: The Cussler Museum contains a collection of more than 100 rare and vintage automobiles, ranging in years from 1906 to 1965. The museum was started by renowned best selling author Clive Cussler. Some of the vehicles on display include a 1906 Stanley Steamer, 1911 Locomobile, 1913 Marmon and many more. **SEASON & HOURS**: May thru September, Monday and Tuesday only, 10am to 7pm. **DIRECTIONS**: From I-70 Exit 266 go north 2.3 miles on SR-72/Ward Rd; go west 1.4 miles on SR-72/64th Ave; go north .7 mile on SR-72/Indiana St; go west .1 mile on 69th Ave.

Denver Firefighters Museum
1326 Tremont Pl, Denver CO 80204

WEB SITE: www.denverfirefightersmuseum.org
PHONE: 303-892-1436
COORDINATES: 39.7408 | -104.9926

Museum
History - Local
Fee: $6
Interstate:
I-25 Exit 210A; 1.3 miles
Facilities:
Gift Shop

DESCRIPTION: The Denver Firefighters Museum preserves the history of the Denver Fire Department and fire fighting through artifacts, documents, and photographs. Among the exhibits are personal protective tools and equipment, various fire trucks, and educational materials about fire suppression. Visitors can also tour the station's living quarters and learn about the large fires in Denver's history. **SEASON & HOURS**: Open year-round, Monday through Saturday, 10am to 6pm. **DIRECTIONS**: From I-25 Exit 210A go east 1 mile on Colfax Ave, left two blocks on Glenarm Pl, right at 14th St, and right at Tremont Pl.

Denver Museum of Miniatures, Dolls and Toys

1880 Gaylord St, Denver CO 80206

WEB SITE: www.dmmdt.org
PHONE: 303-322-1053
COORDINATES: 39.7462 | -104.9609

DESCRIPTION: The museum encompasses many different cultures in its collections of dolls and miniatures, teaching visitors about these varying customs with an array of permanent and rotating exhibits. Guests can also explore fully furnished miniature houses, miniature trains, planes and cars, giant teddy bears, a miniature circus, antique dolls, and Southwestern homes as they tour the museum. **SEASON & HOURS**: Wednesday through Saturday, 10am to 4pm; Sunday, 1pm to 4pm. **DIRECTIONS**: From I-70 Exit 276A go south 1.8 miles on Steele St, west .6 mile on 26th Ave, south .6 mile on Gaylord St.

Museum
Dolls & Toys
Fee: $6
Interstate:
I-70 Exit 276A; 3 miles
Facilities:
Gift Shop
Food

Denver Museum of Nature & Science

2001 Colorado Blvd, Denver CO 80205

WEB SITE: www.dmns.org
PHONE: 303-370-6000
COORDINATES: 39.7474 | -104.9408

DESCRIPTION: The Denver Museum of Nature and Science has a number of different activities to occupy your time while visiting. Exhibitions include Body Worlds, Discovery Zone for Kids, Photographs from an Amazon Journey, Egyptian Mummies, Odyssey of the Stars, Native American Cultures, Gems and Minerals, Prehistoric Journey, and several Wildlife exhibits. The IMAX theater is open to visitors and offers interesting, educational films, as does the Planetarium. **SEASON & HOURS**: Daily, 9am to 5pm. **DIRECTIONS**: From I-70 Exit 276B go south 2.1 miles on Colorado Blvd.

Museum
Science
Fee: $11
Interstate:
I-70 Exit 276B; 2.1 miles
Facilities:
Visitor Center
Gift Shop
Picnic Area
Food

Dillon Schoolhouse Museum

403 La Bonte St, Dillon CO 80435

WEB SITE: www.summithistorical.org
PHONE: 970-468-2207
COORDINATES: 39.6311 | -106.0430

DESCRIPTION: The inside of the museum is a replica of how the Dillon school appeared at the turn-of-the-century and has a full complement of schoolroom tools used at that time. Adjacent to the schoolhouse are the general store and blacksmith shop, which also house a number of artifacts. **SEASON & HOURS**: Open year-round, Tuesday through Saturday, 1pm to 4pm in summer; Saturday only 1pm to 4pm in winter. **DIRECTIONS**: From I-70 Exit 205 follow US-6 east for 1.1 miles; turn right at Lake Dillon Dr; left at Tenderfoot St .2 mile; right at La Bonte St to destination.

Museum
History - Local
Fee: $6
Interstate:
I-70 Exit 205; 1.5 miles
Facilities:
Gift Shop

Dinosaur Journey Museum

550 Jurassic Ct, Fruita CO 81521

WEB SITE: www.wcmuseum.org
PHONE: 970-858-7282
COORDINATES: 39.1517 | -108.7389

DESCRIPTION: The museum was designed with kids in mind and includes a dinosaur reading library, a sandbox where children can make their own dinosaur tracks, a simulated earthquake ride, and a "quarry site" where kids have the chance to dig up some real dinosaur bones from the Jurassic Period. Other interactive exhibits allow visitors to view and compare real bones, casts, and robotic reconstructions of different dinosaurs. **SEASON & HOURS**: Year-round, daily, 9am to 5pm. **DIRECTIONS**: From I-70 Exit 19 go south .2 mile on SR-340 then right at Jurassic Ct.

Museum
Children's
Fee: $7
Interstate:
I-70 Exit 19; .2 mile
Facilities:
Gift Shop

Dinosaur National Monument

4545 E Highway 40, Dinosaur CO 81610

WEB SITE: www.nps.gov/dino/
PHONE: 970-374-3000
COORDINATES: 40.2448 | -108.9735

DESCRIPTION: Dinosaur National Monument contains dinosaur fossils, petroglyphs, pictographs, scenic vistas, and historic homesites. Dinosaur fossils can only be seen in the Utah portion of the park about 7 miles north of Jensen, Utah, on SR-149. The Monument also offers auto tour routes, hiking, fishing, boating, picnicking, and camping. **SEASON & HOURS**: The Monument is open year-round. The Utah visitor center is open daily 8:30am to 4:30pm. The Colorado visitor center is open March through October, 8:30am to 4:30pm, daily in summer, Wednesday through Sunday rest of year. **DIRECTIONS**: The Colorado entrance to the Monument is 2 miles east of Dinosaur on US-40.

Outdoors
Park / Recreation Area
Fee: Free
Facilities:
Visitor Center
Picnic Area
Camping

Dinosaur Ridge

16831 W Alameda Pkwy, Morrison CO 80465

WEB SITE: www.dinoridge.org
PHONE: 303-697-3466
COORDINATES: 39.6881 | -105.1907

DESCRIPTION: Dinosaur Ridge is a geologically famous National Natural Landmark and is on the State Register of Historic Places. The site preserves over 300 dinosaur footprints, bones, and fossils of prehistoric insects and plants. A self-guided tour includes sixteen interpretative signs that describe fossil remains and other features of the area. Guided tours are also available. **SEASON & HOURS**: Open daily year-round; 10am to 4:30pm in summer; 10am to 3:30pm other seasons. **DIRECTIONS**: From I-70 Exit 260 go south 1.8 miles on SR-470 then west .1 mile on Alameda Pkwy.

Attraction
Educational
Fee: Self-guided tours are free
Interstate:
I-70 Exit 260; 1.9 miles
Facilities:
Visitor Center
Gift Shop
Picnic Area
Food

Discovery Museum at the Powerhouse

1333 Camino Del Rio, Durango CO 81301

WEB SITE: www.durangodiscovery.org
PHONE: 970-259-9234
COORDINATES: 37.2788 | -107.8793

Museum
Science
Fee: Call
Facilities:
Gift Shop
Food

DESCRIPTION: What once used to be a children's museum is now an interactive museum that showcases exhibits for all ages. The Discovery Museum works to educate children about the power of the past, present, and future, giving them a head start in a society that is moving at such a fast pace. An emphasis is placed on teaching visitors about the new, "greener" energy of the future. **SEASON & HOURS**: Grand opening Fall 2010. Open year-round, Wednesday through Saturday, 10am to 5pm; Sunday, 1pm to 5pm. **DIRECTIONS**: In downtown Durango near the intersection of Main Ave and 14th St.

Durango & Silverton Narrow Gauge Railroad & Museum

479 Main Ave, Durango CO 81301

WEB SITE: www.durangotrain.com
PHONE: 970-247-2733 or 877-872-4607
COORDINATES: 37.2704 | -107.8834

Attraction
Cable, Cog, Incline, Train
Rides
Fee: $81 to $169
Facilities:
Gift Shop
Food

DESCRIPTION: The Durango & Silverton is a 45-mile trip along the Animas River in the San Juan Mountains. Established in 1881, this historic train has been in continuous operation for nearly 130 years, carrying passengers behind vintage steam locomotives and rolling stock indigenous to the line. Passengers are taken from Durango to Silverton where there is a 2-hour 15-minute layover for touring and shopping. The round-trip ride is about 9 hours long. **SEASON & HOURS**: May to October; train departures vary from 8:15am to 9:45pm. **DIRECTIONS**: On the west side of town at the intersection of US-550 and College Dr.

Elbert County Historical Society and Museum

515 Comanche St, Kiowa CO 80117

WEB SITE: www.elbertcountymuseum.org
PHONE: 303-621-2088
COORDINATES: 39.3467 | -104.4612

Museum
History - Local
Fee: Free (donations accepted)
Interstate:
I-70 Exit 352; 36 miles or
I-25 Exit 182; 24 miles
Facilities:
Gift Shop

DESCRIPTION: Visitors can learn about the history of Elbert County through a permanent exhibit that traces the lives of the Plains Indians, traders and trappers, and the settlers. A number of rotating exhibits teach visitors about the scenery and animals of prehistoric Elbert County and the tragic effect the 1930's had on Elbert County. A replica of Main Street allows visitors to experience a typical turn-of-the-century plains town. **SEASON & HOURS**: Memorial Day to Labor Day, Thursday through Sunday, 1pm to 4pm. **DIRECTIONS**: From I-70 Exit 352 follow SR-86 west 36 miles. From I-25 Exit 182 follow SR-86 east 24 miles.

Fort Garland Museum
29477 Highway 159, Fort Garland CO 81133

WEB SITE: www.coloradohistory.org/hist_sites/ft_Garland/ft_garland.htm
PHONE: 791-379-3512
COORDINATES: 37.4246 | -105.4313

DESCRIPTION: While exploring the restored fort, visitors can view exhibits displaying some of the West's famous mountain-men. If visitors have time, they can travel to Pike's Stockade on the Conejos River, where Pike and his men spent the winter of 1806. Guided tours are offered for those who want to learn more about the fort. **SEASON & HOURS**: April through October, daily, 9am to 5pm. November through March, Thursday through Monday, 10am to 4pm. **DIRECTIONS**: From I-25 Exit 50 follow US-160 west 47.8 miles then SR-159 south .2 mile.

> *Museum*
>   *History - Local*
> **Fee**: $5
> **Interstate**:
>   I-25 Exit 50; 48 miles
> **Facilities**:
>   Gift Shop

Fort Lupton Museum
453 First St, Fort Lupton CO 80621

WEB SITE: www.fortlupton.org/museum.htm
PHONE: 303-857-1634
COORDINATES: 40.0802 | -104.8132

DESCRIPTION: While visiting the museum, you can learn about the people who have lived in and around the Fort Lupton area since 1836, view the arrow-head collection donated by Ralph Haynes in 1950, and examine an assortment of old photographs of Fort Lupton. **SEASON & HOURS**: Year-round, Monday through Friday, 9am to Noon, 1pm to 4pm. **DIRECTIONS**: From I-25 Exit 235 follow SR-52 east for 9 miles or from I-76 Exit 31 follow SR-52 west for 9 miles.

> *Museum*
>   *History - Local*
> **Fee**: $5
> **Interstate**:
>   I-25 Exit 235; 9 miles or
>   I-76 Exit 31; 9 miles

Fort Morgan Museum
414 Main St, Fort Morgan CO 80701

WEB SITE: www.cityoffortmorgan.com/index.aspx?NID=238
PHONE: 970-542-4010
COORDINATES: 40.2515 | -103.8014

DESCRIPTION: The museum explores the many facets of Fort Morgan history, from prehistoric times up through modern day. There is a little bit of everything offered, with exhibits displaying information on natural history, archaeology, transportation, schools, emigration, and Native American artifacts. The museum also offers monthly lectures and an art show during the summer months. **SEASON & HOURS**: Monday and Friday, 10am to 5pm; Tuesday through Thursday, 10am to 8pm; Saturday, 11am to 5pm. **DIRECTIONS**: From I-76 Exit 80 go south .8 mile on SR-52/Main St.

> *Museum*
>   *History - Local*
> **Fee**: Free
> **Interstate**:
>   I-76 Exit 80; .8 mile
> **Facilities**:
>   Gift Shop

Fort Sedgwick Museum
114 E 1st, Julesburg CO 80737

WEB SITE: http://users.kci.net/history/
PHONE: 970-474-2061
COORDINATES: 40.9869 | -102.2615

DESCRIPTION: The Fort Sedgwick Museum contains interpretive displays featuring the stories of Fort Sedgwick, the town of Julesburg, and the history of northeastern Colorado. A research room is also available to visitors in the museum. Southwest of the museum on 1st St is the Depot Museum, which houses relics documenting the early pioneer life. **SEASON & HOURS**: Year-round, Monday through Friday, 9am to 1pm (4pm in summer). The Depot Museum is open only in summer. **DIRECTIONS**: From I-76 Exit 180 follow US-385 north 1.9 miles then turn left (west) on 1st St and follow .6 mile. The Depot Museum is also on 1st St about .2 miles southwest of the Fort Sedgwick Museum.

Museum
History - Local
Fee: $1
Interstate:
I-76 Exit 180; 2.5 miles
Facilities:
Gift Shop

Fort Uncompahgre History Museum
205 Gunnison River Dr, Delta CO 81416

WEB SITE: www.colorado.com/Listing.aspx?did=332
PHONE: 970-874-1718
COORDINATES: 38.7489 | -108.0737

DESCRIPTION: Fort Uncompahgre was established as a fur trading post in the 1820's by Antoine Robidoux near the present site of Delta, Colorado. The museum consists of seven re-created cabins on the banks of the Gunnison River. **SEASON & HOURS**: April through September, daily, 9am to 3pm. **DIRECTIONS**: From I-70 Exit 26 follow US-50 south 44.4 miles then go west .2 mile on Gunnison River Rd.

Museum
History - Local
Fee: $4
Interstate:
I-70 Exit 26; 44.6 miles
Facilities:
Gift Shop

Fort Vasquez Museum
13412 US Highway 85, Platteville CO 80651

WEB SITE: www.coloradohistory.org/hist_sites/ft_vasquez/ft_vasquez.htm
PHONE: 970-785-2832
COORDINATES: 40.1949 | -104.8208

DESCRIPTION: Visitors can tour the 1835 fur trading post excavated and restored in 1968-1970. The museum on site houses 4,000 artifacts found during the excavation process in addition to exhibits which follow the lives of Louis Vasquez, Andrew Sublette, and the mountain-men they employed to work the fort. **SEASON & HOURS**: Summer: Monday through Saturday, 9:30am to 4:30pm; Sunday, 1pm to 4:30pm. Winter: Wednesday through Saturday, 9:30am to 4:30pm; Sunday, 9am to 4:30pm. **DIRECTIONS**: From I-25 Exit 243 go east 8.4 miles on SR-60 then south .8 mile on US-85.

Museum
History - Local
Fee: $1
Interstate:
I-25 Exit 243; 9.2 miles
Facilities:
Gift Shop

Francisco Fort Museum
306 Main St, La Veta CO 81055

WEB SITE: www.kmitch.com/Huerfano/franfort.html
PHONE: 719-742-5501
COORDINATES: 37.5077 | -105.0090

DESCRIPTION: Established to provide protection against the threat of Indian attack, the fort now serves as a museum housing a number of artifacts collected through local donations. Artifacts are arranged in rooms based on the time period they originated from. Three other historic buildings (the Ritter schoolhouse, the Saloon, and a log building used as a blacksmith's workshop) are also located on the premises. **SEASON & HOURS**: Summer, daily, 9am to 5pm. **DIRECTIONS**: From I-25 Exit 50 follow US-160 west 21.2 miles then SR-12 south 4.7 miles.

> *Museum*
>   *History - Local*
> **Fee**: Free (donations accepted)
> **Interstate**:
>   I-25 Exit 50; 25.9 miles
> **Facilities**:
>   Gift Shop

Fred Harman Art Museum
85 Harman Park Dr, Pagosa Springs CO 81147

WEB SITE: www.harmanartmuseum.com
PHONE: 970-731-5785
COORDINATES: 37.2673 | -107.0526

DESCRIPTION: On display are the works of Fred Harman, a native of Pagosa Springs, who used his experiences working as a cowboy as inspiration for his art. The self-taught artist, who also happened to work with Walt Disney for a year before the pair went their separate ways, created the Red Ryder and Little Beaver comic strip. This comic strip became the largest syndicated comic in the country after being in circulation from 1938-1964. **SEASON & HOURS**: Summer: Monday through Saturday, 10:30am to 5pm; Sunday, Noon to 4pm. Winter: Monday through Friday, 10:30am to 5pm. **DIRECTIONS**: From Pagosa Springs follow US-160 west for 2.7 miles.

> *Museum*
>   *Art / Art Gallery*
> **Fee**: $4
> **Facilities**:
>   Gift Shop

Frisco Historic Park and Museum
120 E Main St, Frisco CO 80443

WEB SITE: www.townoffrisco.com/activities/historic-park-museum/
PHONE: 970-668-3428
COORDINATES: 39.5754 | -106.1005

DESCRIPTION: Set on the expansive grounds of the Frisco Historical Park, the museum is made up of a collection of buildings, each showing some aspect of Frisco's colorful history. Through displays such as the Women's Exhibit, the train and town of Frisco diorama, the schoolhouse museum, and other historic artifacts from the town, visitors are given a broad view of what the town was like in the past. The Park and Museum also host regular lectures, guided hikes, and tours. **SEASON & HOURS**: October through April, Tuesday through Saturday, 10am to 4pm; Sunday, 10am to 2pm. May through September, Tuesday through Saturday, 9am to 5pm; Sunday 9am to 3pm. **DIRECTIONS**: From I-70 Exit 201 follow Main St east for .6 mile.

> *Museum*
>   *History - Local*
> **Fee**: Free
> **Interstate**:
>   I-70 Exit 201; .6 mile
> **Facilities**:
>   Picnic Area

Galloping Goose Historical Society
421 Railroad Ave, Dolores CO 81327

WEB SITE: www.gallopinggoose5.com
PHONE: 970-882-7082
COORDINATES: 37.4734 | -108.5034

Museum
Railroad / Trains
Fee: Free
Facilities:
Gift Shop

DESCRIPTION: The Galloping Goose Historical Society manages the Rio Grande Southern Railroad Museum. The museum collection includes pictures (many one-of-a-kind), interpretive displays, artwork, models, reference books and papers, plus numerous artifacts. On display in front of the museum is the famous Rio Grande Southern Railroad Galloping Goose Number 5. **SEASON & HOURS**: Mid-May to mid-October, Monday through Saturday, 9am to 5pm. Mid-October to mid-May, Tuesday and Thursday, 10am to 2pm. **DIRECTIONS**: In town at SR-145 and 5th St.

The Gateway Colorado Auto Museum
43224 Highway 141, Gateway CO 81522

WEB SITE: www.gatewayautomuseum.com
PHONE: 970-931-2895
COORDINATES: 38.6780 | -108.9813

Museum
Vehicles
Fee: $9
Facilities:
Gift Shop

DESCRIPTION: The museum has a collection of over 40 cars, aligned in a timeline, designed to show how the American car has evolved over the decades. Several other exhibits are arranged to show early American cars, the most stylish cars of the 1930's, muscle cars, and a 1954 Oldsmobile F-88 Concept Car. **SEASON & HOURS**: Wednesday through Sunday, 10am to 5pm. **DIRECTIONS**: From I-70 Exit 37 go south on I-70-BUS 1.2 miles then follow SR-141 southwest for 51.5 miles.

Georgetown Energy Museum
600 Griffith St, Georgetown CO 80444

WEB SITE: www.georgetownenergymuseum.org
PHONE: 303-569-3557
COORDINATES: 39.7061 | -105.6952

Museum
History - Local
Fee: Free (donations accepted)
Interstate:
I-70 Exit 228; .8 mile

DESCRIPTION: The museum is located in Georgetown's fully-functioning Hydroelectric generating plant, which has been in operation since 1900. The museum provides a general history about hydroelectric power as well as several exhibits displaying photography and household appliances used in the late 19th and early 20th century. **SEASON & HOURS**: June through September, Monday through Saturday, 10am to 4pm; Sunday, Noon to 4pm. **DIRECTIONS**: From I-70 Exit 228 go east on 15th St, turn right on Argentine St and follow .6 mile then turn left onto 7th St and follow .2 mile to Griffith St and turn right.

The Gilpin History Museum
228 High St, Central City CO 80427

WEB SITE: www.gilpinhistory.org
PHONE: 303-582-5283
COORDINATES: 39.8010 | -105.5110

Museum
History - Local
Fee: $5
Interstate:
I-70 Exit 243; 8.4 miles
Facilities:
Gift Shop

DESCRIPTION: Contains items related to Gilpin's most thriving era. Included in the permanent exhibit are a Victorian-style parlor, dining room and kitchen, a carpenter's shop, a doctor's office, and a schoolroom as well as children's toys and clothes, an antique lamp collection, a display of fire fighting apparatus and artifacts, and salon exhibit. The museum also includes the re-creation of a typical main street. **SEASON & HOURS**: Summer, daily, 11am to 4pm. **DIRECTIONS**: From I-70 Exit 243 follow the Central City Pkwy 8.1 miles; turn left on Spruce St and follow .2 miles; turn right onto E 1st High St and follow .1 mile. (Use caution as streets can be narrow.)

Grande River Vineyards
787 Elberta Ave, Palisade CO 81526

WEB SITE: www.granderiverwines.com
PHONE: 970-464-5867 or 800-264-7696
COORDINATES: 39.1173 | -108.3599

Attraction
Wineries
Fee: Free
Interstate:
I-70 Exit 42
Facilities:
Gift Shop
Lodging

DESCRIPTION: Western Colorado's moderate winters and arid climate make for near-perfect grape-growing conditions. Established in 1990, Grande River Vineyard harvests the largest grape crop in Colorado each year. The winery and vineyard, nestled beneath the Bookcliffs, produces 7,000 to 8,000 cases of wine annually. Outdoor concerts and events take place during summer months. **SEASON & HOURS**: Open daily year-round, 9am to 5pm. **DIRECTIONS**: I-70 Exit 42, just south of exit.

Greeley History Museum
714 8th St, Greeley CO 80631

WEB SITE: www.greeleymuseums.com
PHONE: 970-350-9220
COORDINATES: 40.4248 | -104.6899

Museum
History - Local
Fee: Free
Interstate:
I-25 Exit 257A; 19 miles
Facilities:
Gift Shop

DESCRIPTION: Housed in a building listed on the National Register of Historic Places, the Greeley History Museum provides visitors with a look at Greeley's history beginning from its earliest human inhabitants up through the days of cowboys and the Wild West. Among the important figures presented at the museum are The Meekers, Rattlesnake Kate, Dr. Ella Mead, and P.T. Barnum. **SEASON & HOURS**: Wednesday through Friday, 8:30am to 4:30pm; Saturday, 10am to 4pm. **DIRECTIONS**: From I-25 Exit 257A go east 16.4 miles on US-34 then north on US-85-BUS for 2.6 miles; turn right at 8th St (museum is on the south side of street).

Gunnison Pioneer & Train Museum

803 E Tomichi Ave, Gunnison CO 81230

WEB SITE: www.pioneertrainmuseum.org
PHONE: 970-641-4530
COORDINATES: 38.5444 | -106.9176

> *Museum*
>   *History - Local*
> **Fee**: $7

DESCRIPTION: The museum grounds consist of eighteen buildings, all exhibiting artifacts that date back to the early settlers of Gunnison County. Other displays range from old cars and covered wagons to a narrow gauge train which includes a flanger, a gondola, a boxcar, a livestock car and a caboose. In summer, Jeep tours are available to visit the historical Aberdeen Quarry, which is just a few miles from Gunnison. **SEASON & HOURS**: Open Memorial Day through September; call for hours. **DIRECTIONS**: East end of town on US-50 at Adams St.

Hard Tack Mine

PO Box 94, Lake City CO 81235

WEB SITE: www.hardtackmine.com
PHONE: 970-944-2506
COORDINATES: 38.0194 | -107.3577

> *Attraction*
>   *Historic Site*
> **Fee**: $10
> **Facilities**:
>   Gift Shop

DESCRIPTION: Hard Tack Mine, owned and operated by a former hard rock miner, features 40-minute tours that demonstrate how miners blasted through rock using hand tools and dynamite. More than 100 years old, the mine was made by employees of the Hidden Treasure Mine Company. The mine produced more than a million and a half dollars in silver ore. The area surrounding the mine was once a bustling little community from the 1890's until 1930. **SEASON & HOURS**: Memorial Day to Labor Day, Tuesday through Saturday, 10am to 5pm. **DIRECTIONS**: From Lake City follow CR-20 (Engineer Pass Rd) west for 2.5 miles.

Hiwan Homestead Museum

4208 S Timbervale Dr, Evergreen CO 80439

WEB SITE: www.jeffco.us/openspace/openspace_T56_R10.htm
PHONE: 720-497-7650
COORDINATES: 39.6390 | -105.3238

> *Museum*
>   *History - Local*
> **Fee**: Free
> **Interstate**:
>   I-70 Exit 251 or
>   I-70 Exit 252; 7 miles

DESCRIPTION: Hiwan Homestead Museum was originally the home to which several generations of Colorado's aristocratic society retired during the summer months. It was added to the National Register of Historic Places due to its unique architecture known as the Rocky Mountain Rustic style. The reconstructed rooms of the house are representative of the comfortable style often seen in early mountain summer homes. The museum also offers crafts and interactive programs. **SEASON & HOURS**: June through August, Tuesday through Sunday, 11am to 5pm. September through May, Tuesday through Sunday, Noon to 5pm. **DIRECTIONS**: *Westbound Travelers*: From I-70 Exit 252 go south 6.4 miles on SR-74 (Evergreen Pkwy); turn left at Douglas Park Rd .3 mile; turn left at Pine Dr then continue on Meadow Dr to Timberbale Dr and turn left. *Eastbound Travelers*: From I-70 Exit 251 follow US-40 east .5 mile then follow directions provided for westbound travelers.

InfoZone News Museum
100 E Abriendo Ave, Pueblo CO 81004

WEB SITE: www.infozonenewsmuseum.com
PHONE: 719-562-5604
COORDINATES: 38.2594 | -104.6206

Museum
History - Local
Fee: Free
Interstate:
I-25 Exit 97B; .6 mile
Facilities:
Gift Shop

DESCRIPTION: Located on the fourth floor of the Rawlings Public Library in Pueblo, the news museum works to increase public knowledge about the freedom of speech and press, the history of Pueblo, and the newspapers of Colorado. Interactive exhibits include a demonstration of how newspapers were produced before computers. New exhibits come to the InfoZone News Museum monthly. Independent films are often shown in the museum's 100-seat movie theater. **SEASON & HOURS**: Year-round, Monday through Thursday, 9am to 9pm; Friday and Saturday, 9am to 6pm; Sunday, 1pm to 5pm. **DIRECTIONS**: From I-25 Exit 97B go west .6 mile on Abriendo Ave.

The Jack Dempsey Museum
412 Main St, Manassa CO 81141

WEB SITE: http://museumtrail.org/jackdempseymuseum.asp
PHONE: 719-843-5207
COORDINATES: 37.1737 | -105.9359

Museum
Sports
Fee: Free
Facilities:
Gift Shop

DESCRIPTION: Extremely proud of their most famous figure, the town of Manassa created a museum in honor of Jack Dempsey, the heavyweight boxer, located in the cabin where he was born. The museum contains Dempsey memorabilia, including a pair of gloves he wore while boxing in New York, and numerous photographs. **SEASON & HOURS**: Memorial Day through Labor Day, Tuesday through Saturday, 9am to 5pm. **DIRECTIONS**: In town at 4th St and Main St. Manassa is 24 miles south of Alamosa.

James Underhill Museum
1416 Miner St, Idaho Springs CO 80452

WEB SITE: www.historicidahosprings.com/attractions/underhill_museum.php
PHONE: 303-567-4709
COORDINATES: 39.7418 | -105.5176

Museum
History - Local
Fee: Free
Interstate:
I-70 Exit 240; .2 mile

DESCRIPTION: The James Underhill museum, once the home of James Underhill and his wife Lucy, gives visitors the chance to enjoy an early 20th century home while exploring the mining and mineral exhibits on display. Lucy Underhill's Victorian Garden and Courtyard is also on display in the back of the museum. **SEASON & HOURS**: June through September, daily, 10am to 4pm. **DIRECTIONS**: From I-70 Exit 240 go north on Chicago Creek Rd/13th Ave and turn right one block at Miner St.

Johnstown Parish House Museum

701 Charlotte St, Johnstown CO 80534

WEB SITE: www.jhs1.netfirms.com
PHONE: 970-587-0278
COORDINATES: 40.3361 | -104.9140

Museum
History - Local
Fee: Free
Interstate:
I-25 Exit 252; 3.6 miles

DESCRIPTION: The upstairs of the Johnstown Parish Home Museum is furnished to show how an early 1900's home would have appeared in the small town. In the lower levels of the home are exhibits displaying the agricultural history of Johnstown, the importance of the Great Western Sugar Factory, and items pioneers brought west with them. A collection of graduation pictures from the classes of Johnstown and a sealed time capsule can also be seen. **SEASON & HOURS**: Open year-round on Wednesdays from 9am to Noon and the first Saturday of every month from 9am to Noon. **DIRECTIONS**: From I-25 Exit 252 go east 3.5 miles on SR-60 then turn left onto Fremont Ave and left onto Charlotte St.

Kauffman House Museum

Pitkin and Lake Avenue, Grand Lake CO 80447

WEB SITE: www.kauffmanhouse.org
PHONE: 970-627-9644
COORDINATES: 40.2508 | -105.8180

Museum
History - Local
Fee: $3
Facilities:
Gift Shop

DESCRIPTION: The Kauffman House Museum preserves the only remaining log hotel built in Grand Lake prior to 1900. The museum houses a diverse collection of artifacts including books, quilts, clothing, furniture, iron kitchenware, postcards, paintings, and photographs. The museum also explores the histories of the Kauffman family and the later owners of the hotel. **SEASON & HOURS**: Memorial Day through Labor Day, daily, 11am to 5pm; open weekends in September, 11am to 5pm. **DIRECTIONS**: In town at Pitkin St and Lake Ave.

Lafayette Miners Museum

108 E Simpson St, Lafayette CO 80026

WEB SITE: www.cityoflafayette.com/Page.asp?NavID=802
PHONE: 303-665-7030
COORDINATES: 39.9982 | -105.0895

Museum
History - Local
Fee: Free
Interstate:
I-25 Exit 229; 6 miles

DESCRIPTION: The Museum, originally known as the Lewis Home, was used as both a home for miners in the 1890's and as a meeting place for them while they were on strike from 1913-1915. It offers visitors the chance to view a wide variety of subjects including the history of Lafayette, a collection of unusual household artifacts, an extensive collection of mining tools and equipment, and a "school room," which traces the educational past of Lafayette. **SEASON & HOURS**: Thursday and Saturday, 2pm to 4pm. **DIRECTIONS**: From I-25 Exit 229 go west 5.8 miles on SR-7/Baseline Rd; south .1 mile on Public Rd; east one block on Simpson St.

Leanin' Tree Museum and Sculpture Garden of Western Art

6055 Longbow Drive, Boulder CO 80301

WEB SITE: www.leanintreemuseum.com/
PHONE: 800-525-0656
COORDINATES: 40.0645 | -105.2140

Museum	
Art / Art Gallery	
Fee: Free	
Interstate:	
I-25 Exit 235; 13.6 miles	
Facilities:	
Gift Shop	

DESCRIPTION: Features fine art paintings and bronzes of western America created after 1930. The collection consists of cowboys, Indians, wildlife and landscapes. There are 250 paintings and 150 bronze sculptures created by more than 100 artists on display. **SEASON & HOURS**: Open year-round except holidays, Monday thru Friday, 8am to 5pm; Saturday and Sunday, 10am to 5pm. **DIRECTIONS**: From I-25 Exit 235, go 11.2 miles west on SR-52 to SR-119. Turn left (southwest) on SR-119 1.3 miles, then south on 63rd Street .7 mile, and west .4 mile on Longbow Drive.

Limon Heritage Museum

899 1st St, Limon CO 80828

WEB SITE: www.ourjourney.info/MyJourneyDestinations/LimonHeritageMuseum.asp
PHONE: 719-775-8605
COORDINATES: 39.2607 | -103.6878

Museum	
History - Local	
Fee: Free	
Interstate:	
I-70 Exit 361; 1.1 miles	
Facilities:	
Picnic Area	

DESCRIPTION: The museum complex is comprised of Limon Depot, Exhibit Building, and Railroad Park. As visitors walk through the Depot, they will be introduced to a life on the plains with exhibits like the Houtz Native American Collection, a one-room prairie schoolhouse, and a permanent "trains of the plains" exhibit. The journey continues in the Exhibit Building as visitors explore an old store, barbershop, and prairie kitchen. A collection of photographs give life to the plains of the 1900's. **SEASON & HOURS**: Memorial Day through Labor Day, Monday through Saturday, 1pm to 8pm. **DIRECTIONS**: From I-70 Exit 361 go west .8 mile on US-24/Main St; south .1 mile on B St; west .2 mile on 1st St.

Lowell Thomas Museum

3rd & Victor Avenue, Victor CO 80860

WEB SITE: www.victorcolorado.com/museum.htm
PHONE: 719-689-5509
COORDINATES: 38.7099 | -105.1401

Museum	
History - Local	
Fee: $4	
Interstate:	
I-25 Exit 141; 49 miles	
Facilities:	
Gift Shop	

DESCRIPTION: The history of the gold rush, the stories of the pioneers involved, and the tools they used are the main focus of the Lowell Thomas Museum. Also included are artifacts that once belonged to the famous journalist, household items, Victorian-style rooms and a doctor's office, and a large collection of local photographs and newspapers. Visitors can also pan for gold and gems outside the museum and tour an old gold mine.
SEASON & HOURS: Memorial Day through Labor Day, Wednesday through Sunday, 9am to 5pm. **DIRECTIONS**: From I-25 Exit 141 follow US-24 east for 25 miles then follow SR-67 south for 24 miles.

MacGregor Ranch and Museum
180 MacGregor Ln, Estes Park CO 80517

WEB SITE: www.macgregorranch.org
PHONE: 970-586-3479
COORDINATES: 40.3941 | -105.5212

DESCRIPTION: Founded in 1873, MacGregor Ranch is the last remaining working cattle ranch in Estes Park. Its historic collection and structures are original to the homestead family, and its collection is completely intact. The attraction offers self guided tours of the museum, milkhouse, smokehouse, blacksmith shop and horse-drawn machinery exhibits. The ranch also offers all-natural beef products for sale. **SEASON & HOURS**: June through August, Tuesday through Sunday, 10am to 4pm. **DIRECTIONS**: From I-25 Exit 243 go west 36.5 miles on SR-66 and US-36 then travel north 1.2 miles on MacGregor Ave and MacGregor Ln.

> *Museum*
>   *History - Local*
> **Fee**: $3
> **Interstate**:
>   I-25 Exit 243; 37.7 miles
> **Facilities**:
>   Gift Shop

The Madden Museum of Art
6363 S Fiddler's Green Cir, Greenwood Village CO 80111

WEB SITE: www.themaddenmuseum.org
PHONE: 303-763-1970
COORDINATES: 39.6022 | -104.8928

DESCRIPTION: The Madden Museum of Art features an extensive gallery from the personal collection of a local businessman and his wife. The collection includes a number of pieces by well-known artists and the more obscure. Other collections presented at the museum are on loan from different collectors. The museum is located on the atrium level of the Palazzo Verdi building in the Denver Tech Center. **SEASON & HOURS**: Year-round, Monday through Friday, 9am to 5pm. **DIRECTIONS**: From I-25 Exit 197 go west .5 mile on Arapahoe Rd then north .5 mile on Greenwood Plaza Blvd and turn right at Fiddler's Green Cir for .1 mile.

> *Museum*
>   *Art / Art Gallery*
> **Fee**: Free
> **Interstate**:
>   I-25 Exit 197; 1.1 miles
> **Facilities**:
>   Picnic Area
>   Food

Miramont Castle
9 Capitol Hill Ave, Manitou Springs CO 80829

WEB SITE: www.miramontcastle.org
PHONE: 719-685-1011 or 888-685-1011
COORDINATES: 38.8590 | -104.9226

DESCRIPTION: Miramont Castle is over 14,000 square feet and has over 40 rooms built in nine different architectural styles. The mansion has eight-sided rooms, a sixteen-sided room, a solarium that was once a conservatory greenhouse, and a tea room offering lunch and afternoon tea by reservation. Self-guided tours are available. The mansion was added to the National Register of Historic Places in 1977. **SEASON & HOURS**: Open year-round. *Summer*: daily, 9am to 5pm. *Winter*: Tuesday through Saturday, 10am to 4pm; Sunday, Noon to 4pm. **DIRECTIONS**: From I-25 Exit 141 go west 4 miles on US-24 then exit onto US-24-BUS/Manitou Ave and follow 1.5 miles; turn left on Ruxton Ave .2 miles then right on Capitol Hill Ave.

> *Attraction*
>   *Historic Site*
> **Fee**: $8
> **Interstate**:
>   I-25 Exit 141; 5.7 miles
> **Facilities**:
>   Gift Shop
>   Food

Mollie Kathleen Gold Mine

9388 Highway 67, Cripple Creek CO 80813

WEB SITE: www.goldminetours.com
PHONE: 888-291-5689 x9101 or 719-689-2466
COORDINATES: 38.7538 | -105.1605

Attraction
Historic Site
Fee: $15
Interstate: I-25 Exit 141; 42 miles
Facilities: Gift Shop

DESCRIPTION: The Mollie Kathleen Gold Mine is located at 10,000 feet above sea level on the southwest slope of Pikes Peak. On this one-hour guided tour, visitors descend 1,000 feet into the historic gold mine shaft. Visitors learn about the evolution of underground mining methods from 1891 to the present day. Tour guides demonstrate the operation of various air-powered mining equipment including drifter drills, tuggers, slushers, and other machinery. During a portion of the tour, visitors ride aboard an air-powered "Tram-Air-Locomotive." An ore specimen containing some gold is given to each visitor before the end of the tour. **SEASON & HOURS**: April to late October, 9am to 5pm in summer, 10am to 4pm in spring and fall. **DIRECTIONS**: From I-25 Exit 141 go west 25 miles on US-24 then south 17 miles on SR-67.

Monte Vista National Wildlife Refuge

6120 Highway 15, Monte Vista CO 81144

WEB SITE: www.fws.gov/Refuges/profiles/index.cfm?id=65511
PHONE: 719-589-4021
COORDINATES: 37.4859 | -106.1489

Nature & Wildlife
Wildlife Refuge
Fee: Free

DESCRIPTION: Monte Vista National Wildlife Refuge is located in the heart of Colorado's San Luis Valley. The refuge encompasses nearly 15,000 acres of wetlands and is managed to provide habitat for a wide variety of waterfowl. Mallards, pintail, teal, and Canada geese are common, as are American avocets, killdeer, white-faced ibis, egrets, and herons. Recreational activities include fishing, hunting, photography, and wildlife observation. The refuge also offers self-guided auto and walking tours. **SEASON & HOURS**: Daylight hours, year-round; visitor center open 7:30am to 4pm, Monday thru Friday except on Federal holidays. **DIRECTIONS**: The refuge is located 6 miles south of the town of Monte Vista on SR-15. The visitor center is located at the Alamosa National Wildlife Refuge (4 miles east of Alamosa on US-160 and 2 miles south on El Rancho Ln).

Mountain Bike Hall of Fame

331 Elk Ave, Crested Butte CO 81224

WEB SITE: www.mtnbikehalloffame.com
PHONE: 970-349-6817
COORDINATES: 38.8697 | -106.9844

Museum
Sports
Fee: $3
Facilities: Gift Shop

DESCRIPTION: The Mountain Bike Hall of Fame tells the story of many different bicycle enthusiasts, from the Buffalo Soldiers infantry group to the Morrow Dirt Club from Cupertino California, who were all rumored to be responsible for the creation of the sport of mountain biking. The Hall of Fame honors each of these groups and individuals for their contributions to the development of the sport. The museum also houses a number of vintage bikes, photos, and press clippings from famous races. **SEASON & HOURS**: June through September, daily, 10am to 8pm; December through March, daily, Noon to 6pm. **DIRECTIONS**: In town at the intersection of 4th St and Elk Ave. Crested Butte is 28 miles north of Gunnison via SR-135.

Museum of Colorado Prisons

201 N 1st St, Canon City CO 81212

WEB SITE: www.prisonmuseum.org
PHONE: 719-269-3015
COORDINATES: 38.4390 | -105.2466

> *Museum*
>   *History - Local*
> **Fee**: $7
> **Interstate**:
>   I-25 Exit 101; 36.6 miles
> **Facilities**:
>   Gift Shop

DESCRIPTION: The layout of the museum today is consistent with how the prison appeared when it was under the control of the warden: the upper floor of the museum is lined with inmates' cells, all of which tell the story of Colorado's most infamous prisoners, while the lower floor contains the kitchen, rec room, isolation cells, and dining room. Other artifacts and exhibits on display include the hangman's noose used for the last Colorado hanging, the gas chamber, disciplinary tactics used from 1871 to the present, and inmates' arts and crafts projects. **SEASON & HOURS**: Mid-May to Labor Day, daily, 8:30am to 6pm; Labor Day to mid-October, daily 10am to 5pm; mid-October to mid-May, Wednesday through Sunday, 10am to 5pm. **DIRECTIONS**: From I-25 Exit 101 go west on US-50 36.5 miles then north .1 mile on 1st St.

Museum of Northwest Colorado

590 Yampa Ave, Craig CO 81625

WEB SITE: www.museumnwco.org
PHONE: 970-824-6360
COORDINATES: 40.5158 | -107.5474

> *Museum*
>   *History - Local*
> **Fee**: Free
> **Facilities**:
>   Gift Shop

DESCRIPTION: The Museum of Northwestern Colorado contains a variety of artifacts ranging from old photographs and paintings to a vast collection of cowboy "working artifacts." The museum also has an assortment of Edwin Johnson, Colorado governor and senator, memorabilia and an exhibit displaying the history of and artifacts from the Moffat Railroad. **SEASON & HOURS**: Year-round, Monday through Friday, 9am to 5pm; Saturday, 10am to 4pm. **DIRECTIONS**: In town at the intersection of 6th St and Yampa Ave.

Museum of Outdoor Arts

1000 Englewood Pkwy, Englewood CO 80110

WEB SITE: www.moaonline.org
PHONE: 303-806-0444
COORDINATES: 39.6549 | -104.9986

> *Museum*
>   *Art / Art Gallery*
> **Fee**: Free
> **Interstate**:
>   I-25 Exit 207B; 3.7 miles
> **Facilities**:
>   Picnic Area

DESCRIPTION: The Museum of Outdoor Arts features a variety of exhibits year-round on the second floor of the Englewood Civic Center. Ten sculptures are featured in the Sculpture Garden. The museum also has permanent displays located throughout the city. Walking tour maps and more information about the outdoor gallery is available at the museum. Museum of Outdoor Arts also owns Fiddler's Green Amphitheatre where concerts and events take place throughout the year. **SEASON & HOURS**: Mid-April to mid-August, Monday through Thursday, 9am to 5pm; Friday, 9am to 4pm. **DIRECTIONS**: From I-25 Exit 207B follow US-85 south 3.2 miles then go east .1 mile on Dartmouth and south .4 mile on Inca St.

Museum of Western Colorado

462 Ute Ave, Grand Junction CO 81501

WEB SITE: www.wcmuseum.org
PHONE: 970-242-0971
COORDINATES: 39.0656 | -108.5649

Museum
History - National
Fee: $5.50
Interstate:
I-70 Exit 26; 5.7 miles

DESCRIPTION: The Museum of the West offers a thousand years of history that can be experienced. Visitors can "ride" in a stagecoach, "fly" a 1958 Cessna from Walker Field or see an ancient cup and ladle from the Anasazi. The museum's extensive collection includes interactive exhibits, adobe pottery, a collection of firearms, and audio stations throughout that teach the Ute language. **SEASON & HOURS**: May through September, Monday through Saturday, 9am to 5pm. **DIRECTIONS**: From I-70 Exit 26 follow US-50 south for 5.6 miles then turn left at 5th St and left at Ute Ave.

The National Mining Hall of Fame & Museum

120 W 9th, Leadville CO 80461

WEB SITE: www.leadville.com/MiningMuseum
PHONE: 719-486-1229
COORDINATES: 39.2509 | -106.2939

Museum
History - National
Fee: $7
Interstate:
I-70 Exit 195; 23.3 miles
Facilities:
Gift Shop

DESCRIPTION: The museum features a realistic walk-through replica of a hard-rock mine, which visitors can follow as they learn about the progression of mining technology. Other exhibits include mining dioramas and models, a look at surface and underground coal mining, a gold rush and crystal room, and an exhibit portraying the importance of minerals in our daily lives. The Mining Hall of Fame, found in the museum, pays a tribute to the men and women who were pioneers in the development of discovering and processing the natural resources found. **SEASON & HOURS**: May through October, daily, 9am to 5pm; November through April, daily, 11am to 4pm. **DIRECTIONS**: From I-70 Exit 195 go south 22.2 miles on SR-91; continue .9 mile on US-24/Poplar St; turn right .1 mile on 10th St, left at Harrison Ave, and right on 9th St.

National Renewable Energy Laboratory Visitors Center

15013 Denver West Pkwy, Golden CO 80401

WEB SITE: www.nrel.gov/visitors_center/
PHONE: 303-384-6565
COORDINATES: 39.7404 | -105.1679

Attraction
Educational
Fee: Free
Interstate:
I-70 Exit 263; 0.5 miles
Facilities:
Visitor Center

DESCRIPTION: Visitors can take a self-guided tour through the interactive exhibit hall and learn about energy from the sun, wind, biomass, and other sources of renewable energy. Visitors learn how scientists capture alternative energy resources to produce electricity and fuels. Several outdoor exhibits demonstrate the sun's power. A public reading room is stocked with current information on renewable energy and energy efficiency. **SEASON & HOURS**: Open year-round, Monday through Friday, 9am to 5pm. **DIRECTIONS**: From I-70 Exit 263 go north .1 mile on Denver West Blvd then west .4 mile on Denver West Pkwy.

Old Hundred Gold Mine Tour
PO Box 430, Silverton CO 81433

WEB SITE: www.minetour.com
PHONE: 970-387-5444 or 800-872-3009
COORDINATES: 37.8249 | -107.5857

Attraction
Historic Site
Fee: $16.95
Facilities:
Gift Shop

DESCRIPTION: An electric mine train takes visitors 1,600 feet into Galena Mountain. Visitors walk through tunnels and shafts built by hard-rock miners between 1907 and 1972. Tour guides demonstrate various equipment and techniques used in the mining process. Visitors can also pan for silver and gold before or after mine tours. **SEASON & HOURS**: Mid-May to early October, daily, 10am to 4pm. **DIRECTIONS**: From Silverton follow CR-2 east for 4 miles, turn right at CR-4 for .25 mile, slight left and continue .75 mile on CR-4A

Old Town Museum
420 S 14th St, Burlington CO 80807

WEB SITE: www.burlingtoncolo.com/old-town-museum.htm
PHONE: 719-346-7382 or 800-288-1334
COORDINATES: 39.2983 | -102.2680

Museum
History - Local
Fee: $6
Interstate:
I-70 Exit 438; 1 mile.
Facilities:
Visitor Center
Gift Shop
Food

DESCRIPTION: Old Town Museum is a 6.5-acre complex with 21 buildings restored with authentic artifacts from the turn-of-the-century. Interactive exhibits demonstrate pioneer life on the Colorado prairie. Visitors can ride a horse-drawn wagon to the Kit Carson County Carousel or enjoy ice cream and old-fashioned sodas. **SEASON & HOURS**: Year-round, Monday thru Saturday, 9am to 5pm; Sunday, Noon to 5pm. **DIRECTIONS**: From I-70 Exit 438 travel west .7 miles on US-24/Rose Ave then south .3 mile on 14th St.

Overland Trail Museum
21053 County Road 26.5, Sterling CO 80751

WEB SITE: www.sterlingcolo.com/?page_id=145
PHONE: 970-522-3895
COORDINATES: 40.6182 | -103.1811

Museum
History - National
Fee: $3
Interstate:
I-76 Exit 125; .5 mile

DESCRIPTION: The museum is housed in the original building from 1936 which is made to look like an old fur trading fort. Other buildings on site include a one-room schoolhouse, an Evangelical Lutheran Church, an old general store, barbershop, blacksmith's shop, barn, train depot, and boxcar. A collection of old farming and ranching equipment is kept in the barn as are several pieces of historic printing equipment. Activities that take place annually at the museum include the Prairie School, which runs weekly sessions for six to eight weeks each summer, small weddings, and Sunday morning church services in the country church. **SEASON & HOURS**: April through October, Monday through Sunday, 9am to 5pm; Sunday, 1pm to 5pm. November through March, Monday through Saturday, 10am to 4pm. **DIRECTIONS**: From I-76 Exit 125 go west .5 mile on US-6, turn left onto CR-370 and left at Overland Trail.

Pikes Peak Cog Railway
515 Ruxton Ave, Manitou Springs CO 80829

WEB SITE: www.cograilway.com
PHONE: 719-685-5401 or 800-745-3773
COORDINATES: 38.8558 | -104.9313

Attraction	
Cable, Cog, Incline, Train Rides	

Fee: $33
Interstate: I-25 Exit 141; 6.2 miles
Facilities: Gift Shop, Food

DESCRIPTION: Pikes Peak Cog Railway takes visitors to the top of 14,110-foot Pikes Peak. During the trip up, the conductor entertains visitors with history and facts about the mountain, the region, and the engineering feat of constructing the railway. From the summit, visitors can see four states, numerous front-range cities, and the historic gold camps of Cripple Creek and Victor. Round-trip rides take a little over three hours to complete. **SEASON & HOURS**: Open year-round. Railway runs daily April through October between 8am and 5:20pm. **DIRECTIONS**: From I-25 Exit 141 go west 4 miles on US-24 then exit onto US-24-BUS 1.5 miles and turn left on Ruxton Ave and follow for .7 miles.

Pikes Peak Radio & Electronics Museum
6735 Earl Dr, Colorado Springs CO 80918

WEB SITE: www.pikespeakradiomuseum.com
PHONE: 719-550-5810
COORDINATES: 38.9295 | -104.7966

Museum
Science
Fee: Free
Interstate: I-25 Exit 149; 1.2 miles

DESCRIPTION: On display at the museum are a variety of electronic devices dating from the early 1900's to present day. The main focus of the museum is to teach visitors about the history of these devices as well as the men who made the greatest contributions to their advancement. **SEASON & HOURS**: Year-round, Monday through Friday, 10am to 5pm. **DIRECTIONS**: From I-25 Exit 149 go east .9 mile on Woodmen Rd, south .2 mile on Academy Blvd, west .1 mile on York, and south on Earl Dr.

Pioneer Town Museum
PO Box 906, Cedaredge CO 81413

WEB SITE: www.pioneertown.org
PHONE: 970-856-7554
COORDINATES: 38.8972 | -107.9255

Attraction
Restored Settlement / Village
Fee: $3
Interstate: I-70 Exit 41; 50.7 miles.
Facilities: Visitor Center

DESCRIPTION: Pioneer Town features an old town main street lined with original restored structures filled with historical artifacts. Guided tours take visitors through a country store, a log cabin, a multi-sided grain silo, a saloon, and many other buildings. The site also contains the award-winning Chapel of the Cross, which features a two-story-high cross. Also on the site is a working print and blacksmith shop, the States Mining Museum, and the Sutherland Museum of Indian and Western History. **SEASON & HOURS**: Memorial Day weekend to late September, Monday through Saturday, 10am to 4pm; Sunday, 1pm to 4pm. **DIRECTIONS**: From I-70 Exit 41 follow SR-65 south for 50.7 miles. Pioneer Town Museum is two blocks south of Main St off SR-65.

Pioneer Village Museum
110 E Byers Ave, Hot Sulphur Springs CO 80452

WEB SITE: www.grandcountymuseum.com/CountyMuseum.htm
PHONE: 970-725-3939
COORDINATES: 40.0728 | -106.1006

Museum
History - Local
Fee: $5
Facilities:
Gift Shop

DESCRIPTION: Housed in the Hot Sulphur Springs School, the Pioneer Village Museum displays tools, clothing, and artifacts from Colorado's early pioneer days. Other exhibits include a display tracing the history of the skiing industry back to its roots in Hot Sulphur Springs and a presentation of the important role of women in settling the land. **SEASON & HOURS**: Open year-round. *Summer*: Tuesday through Saturday, 10am to 5pm. *Winter*: Wednesday through Saturday, 10am to 4pm. **DIRECTIONS**: In town at the US-40 and Byers Ave intersection.

Plains Conservation Center
21901 E Hampden Ave, Aurora CO 80013

WEB SITE: www.plainsconservationcenter.org
PHONE: 303-693-3621
COORDINATES: 39.6530 | -104.7350

Outdoors
Natural / Scenic Area
Fee: Free
Interstate:
I-225 Exit 4; 6 miles
Facilities:
Picnic Area

DESCRIPTION: This natural area preserves nearly 8,900 acres of prairie in two different areas, one near the city of Aurora and the other near Strasburg. Currently there are no facilities at the West Bijou site near Strasburg. The Aurora site consists of 1,100 acres and features a nature center, two replicated homesteads, a schoolhouse, blacksmith shop, and a barn. Buildings are furnished with antiques and replicas of the pioneer lifestyle. Also on the property are four Cheyenne-style tipis furnished with replicated artifacts. **SEASON & HOURS**: Open Monday thru Friday year-round and on Saturdays April thru December. **DIRECTIONS**: From I-225 Exit 4 go south .4 mile on SR-83/Park Rd then east 5.6 miles on Hampden Ave.

Rangely Museum Society
150 Kennedy Dr, Rangely CO 81648

WEB SITE: www.rangely.com/Museum.htm
PHONE: 970-675-8476
COORDINATES: 40.0870 | -108.7865

Museum
History - Local
Fee: Free

DESCRIPTION: The museum presents the history of Rangely in three phases: Native American and Prehistory, Pioneer and Ranching, and Energy Development. Also on display in the museum are the oral histories given by the senior citizens of Rangely, the restored jail cell, community hall, school house and camp house, and the thousands of historical photographs donated by Rangely residents. The museum runs several tours a year to the many rock art sites in Rangely. **SEASON & HOURS**: July and August, Monday through Saturday, 10am to 2pm. **DIRECTIONS**: Located at the east end of town off SR-64 at Kennedy Dr.

Red, White & Blue Fire Museum

308 N Main St, Breckenridge CO 80424

WEB SITE: www.breckheritage.com/pages/red-white-blue-fire-museum
PHONE: 800-980-1859
COORDINATES: 39.4857 | -106.0461

Museum
History - Local
Fee: $5
Interstate:
I-70 Exit 203; 10 miles

DESCRIPTION: Formed in 1880, the Breckenridge Fire Department consisted of three companies. They were the Red: The Pioneer Hook and Ladder Company; the White: The Independent Hose Company; and the Blue: The Blue River Hose Company. The all-volunteer fire department was composed of miners, teamsters, saloon keepers, merchants, and others. The current museum displays an original human-powered ladder cart, a restored hose cart as well as fire fighting equipment and uniforms from the first companies. **SEASON & HOURS**: Open June through September, Saturday and Sunday, 11am to 3pm. **DIRECTIONS**: From I-70 Exit 203 go south 9.7 miles on SR-9 then continue south .3 miles on Main St.

Rifle Falls State Park

5775 Highway 325, Rifle CO 81650

WEB SITE: http://parks.state.co.us/Parks/RifleFalls/Pages/RifleFallsHome.aspx
PHONE: 970-625-1607
COORDINATES: 39.6741 | -107.7002

Outdoors
Park / Recreation Area
Fee: $6
Interstate:
I-70 Exit 90; 13.5 miles
Facilities:
Picnic Area
Camping

DESCRIPTION: The falls is a lush area of trees and greenery kept moist by the spray of the triple waterfall. Picnicking near the falls is popular. Limestone caves beneath the falls are open for exploring by visitors. Because of its dramatic setting, many weddings and events have been held at Rifle Falls. A variety of outdoor activities are available including biking, camping, fishing, hiking, hunting, picnicking, cross-country skiing, and snowmobiling. **SEASON & HOURS**: Open year-round, 5am to 10pm; anglers and campers have 24-hour access. **DIRECTIONS**: From I-70 Exit 90, go north 4 miles on SR-13 then northeast 9.5 miles on SR-325.

Rock Ledge Ranch Historic Site

3105 Gateway Rd, Colorado Springs CO 80904

WEB SITE: www.rockledgeranch.com/
PHONE: 719-578-6777
COORDINATES: 38.8773 | -104.8714

Attraction
Historic Site
Fee: $6
Interstate:
I-25 Exit 146; 4 miles
Facilities:
Gift Shop

DESCRIPTION: Rock Ledge Ranch Historic Site is a living history farm and museum depicting life in the Pikes Peak region. Four time periods are represented. The American Indian Area represents Ute and Plains Indians life in the 1700's. The Homestead site depicts pioneer life in the 1860's. The Chambers Farm site tells the story of one family that moved to this location in the 1870's. The Orchard House represents the fourth time period of the early 20th Century and the life of Colorado Springs founder, General William J Palmer. **SEASON & HOURS**: Summer, Wednesday thru Sunday, 10am to 5pm. **DIRECTIONS**: From I-25 Exit 146 go west 2.3 miles on Garden of the Gods Rd then south 1.5 miles on 30th St and turn right at Gateway Rd to site entrance.

Rocky Mountain Dinosaur Resource Center

201 S Fairview St, Woodland Park CO 80863

WEB SITE: www.rmdrc.com
PHONE: 719-686-1820
COORDINATES: 38.9938 | -105.0516

Museum
Animals & Nature
Fee: $11.50
Interstate:
I-25 Exit 141; 17.8 miles
Facilities:
Gift Shop

DESCRIPTION: The Dinosaur Resource Center contains an expansive collection of fossilized animals, life-size restorations and skeletons of dinosaurs, and a working fossil laboratory available for public viewing. The exhibits are continually changing as the center's field researcher's advance their work. There are also a number of interactive exhibits, including a dino dig site and playground, available for children. **SEASON & HOURS**: Year-round, Monday through Saturday, 9am to 6pm; Sunday, 10am to 5pm. **DIRECTIONS**: From I-25 Exit 141 follow US-24 east for 17.8 miles then turn left onto Fairview St.

Saint Stephen's Church

470 Main St, Longmont CO 80501

WEB SITE: www.stvrainhistoricalsociety.org
PHONE: 303-776-1870
COORDINATES: 40.1671 | -105.1024

Museum
History - Local
Fee: Free
Interstate:
I-25 Exit 240; 7.6 miles
Facilities:
Picnic Area

DESCRIPTION: Saint Stephen's Church was built in 1881 as the first home for the congregation of Saint Stephen's Episcopal parish. The congregation of 45 communicants held their first services on Palm Sunday in April, 1882. By 1971 the congregation had outgrown the church. In 1976 the Saint Vrain Historical Society purchased the church and restored it to its original condition. It is presently used as the business office for the Saint Vrain Historical Society. The church is designated a local historic landmark and is also listed on the National Register of Historic Places. **SEASON & HOURS**: Year-round, Monday through Wednesday, 9am to 2:30pm; Thursday, 12:30pm to 2:30pm. **DIRECTIONS**: From I-25 Exit 240 go west 6.6 miles on SR-119 then north 1 mile on Main St.

Salida Museum

406 Highway 50 West, Salida CO 81201

WEB SITE: www.salidachamber.org/museum
PHONE: 719-539-7483
COORDINATES: 38.5243 | -106.0086

Museum
History - Local
Fee: $3

DESCRIPTION: The two-room museum is home to a host of different artifacts including Indian artifacts, household furnishings, art, photographs, mineral specimens and tools associated with railroading, mining, farming and ranching. The museum honors its patronesses, Mrs. Harriet Alexander and Mrs. Byrd Raikes Fuqua, and celebrates the rich history of Salida, Colorado. The museum is available for historical and genealogical research. **SEASON & HOURS**: Memorial Day to Labor Day, daily, 11am to 5pm. **DIRECTIONS**: Located southwest of downtown at the intersection of "I" St and US-50.

Santa's Workshop/North Pole

5050 Pikes Peak Hwy, Cascade CO 80809

WEB SITE: www.santas-colo.com
PHONE: 719-684-9432
COORDINATES: 38.9058 | -104.9781

DESCRIPTION: Santa's Workshop/North Pole is a Christmas-themed family amusement park established in 1956. Christmas music fills the air as visitors browse through the village. At the center of Santa's Workshop is the North Pole, an ice-covered pole that never melts. More than 25 rides and other attractions are throughout the park. Magic shows are shown throughout the day at Santa's Show House. **SEASON & HOURS**: Open mid-May to Christmas Eve, 10am to 5pm. Closed Wednesday and Thursday from late August to late December. **DIRECTIONS**: From I-25 Exit 141 go west 9.4 miles on US-24, turn left at Fountain Ave .4 mile and a slight left onto Pikes Peak Highway for .5 mile.

> *Attraction*
>   *Amusement / Theme Park*
> **Fee**: $17.95
> **Interstate**:
>   I-25 Exit 141; 10.3 miles.
> **Facilities**:
>   Gift Shop
>   Picnic Area

Shelby American Collection

5020 Chaparral Court, Boulder CO 80301

WEB SITE: www.shelbyamericancollection.org
PHONE: 303-516-9565
COORDINATES: 40.0659 | -105.2027

DESCRIPTION: The museum contains a collection of various Shelby American automobiles including 289 Cobras, 427 Cobras, Daytona Coupe, GT40, GT350, and GT500. The museum also features automobilia and various tools on display. **SEASON & HOURS**: Year-round from 10am to 4pm on Saturdays. **DIRECTIONS**: From I-25 Exit 235 go west 11 miles on SR-52; south 1 mile on 71st St; west .7 mile on Lookout Rd; south .4 mile on Spine Rd to Chaparral Ct.

> *Museum*
>   *Vehicles*
> **Fee**: $5
> **Interstate**:
>   I-25 Exit 235; 13.2 miles
> **Facilities**:
>   Gift Shop

Shrine of the Stations of the Cross

PO Box 326, San Luis CO 81152

WEB SITE: www.costillacounty-co.gov/stationsofthecross.html
PHONE: 719-672-3685
COORDINATES: 37.2002 | -105.4259

> *Attraction*
>   *Religious Site*
> **Fee**: Free

DESCRIPTION: The Shrine of the Stations of the Cross was built by the parishioners of the Sangre de Cristo Parish. The Shrine is a place of prayer and solace open to members of all faiths. The Stations of the Cross is a series of life-size sculptures depicting the last hours of Christ's life - His judgment, sufferings, death, and resurrection. The Shrine is located on a mesa in the center of San Luis at the junction of SR-142 and SR-159. **SEASON & HOURS**: Open daily, dawn to dusk. **DIRECTIONS**: San Luis is 64 miles west of I-25 Exit 50 via US-160 and SR-159.

South Park City Museum
100 4th St, Fairplay CO 80440

WEB SITE: www.southparkcity.org
PHONE: 719-836-2387
COORDINATES: 39.2251 | -106.0033

DESCRIPTION: South Park City is an extremely authentic illustration of how a Colorado mining boomtown in the 19th century appeared. Each of the buildings that make up South Park City are set with room decoration and artifacts relevant to the time period. The historical exhibits located in each structure demonstrate the professions, trades and industries that contributed to life in a Colorado mining town. **SEASON & HOURS**: Mid-May to Memorial Day, daily, 9am to 5pm. Memorial Day to Labor Day, daily, 9am to 7pm. Labor Day to mid-October, daily, 10am to 6pm. **DIRECTIONS**: From I-70 Exit 203 go south 32 miles on SR-9.

Museum
  History - Local
Fee: $8
Interstate:
  I-70 Exit 203; 32 miles
Facilities:
  Gift Shop

Stanley Museum of Estes Park
517 Big Thompson Rd, Estes Park CO 80517

WEB SITE: www.stanleymuseum.org
PHONE: 970-577-1903
COORDINATES: 40.3789 | -105.5153

DESCRIPTION: The Stanley Museum of Estes Park is the Colorado branch of a museum by the same name in Maine. Invited by the Stanley Hotel to come to Colorado, the Stanley Museum commemorates the work of the Stanley brothers and the "Stanley Steamer" for which they are best remembered. The museum covers the history and impact of the steam car and also offers ghost story tours as a way of incorporating another facet of the Stanley family's history, the Stanley Hotel. **SEASON & HOURS**: May through October, Monday through Saturday, 10am to 3pm. **DIRECTIONS**: From I-25 Exit 257B follow US-34 west for 33.4 miles.

Museum
  Vehicles
Fee: Free
Interstate:
  I-25 Exit 257B; 33.4 miles
Facilities:
  Gift Shop

Strawberry Park Natural Hot Springs
44200 County Road 36, Steamboat Springs CO 80487

WEB SITE: www.strawberryhotsprings.com
PHONE: 970-879-0342
COORDINATES: 40.5600 | -106.8480

DESCRIPTION: Strawberry Park Hot Springs features pools of 104-degree mineral water. Visitors can also enjoy a massage in one of the private massage huts or a Watsu therapy in the private pool. The park also has lodging available from tent sites and rustic cabins to a renovated train caboose. Hiking and biking trails are in nearby Routt National Forest. **SEASON & HOURS**: Open daily year-round, Sunday through Thursday, 10am to 10:30pm; Friday and Saturday, 10am to midnight. **DIRECTIONS**: From town center travel northeast .4 mile on 7th St, continue east .3 mile on Missouri Ave, go north .2 mile on Park Rd and turn right at Strawberry Park Rd .8 mile then continue north on CR-36 for 5.1 miles.

Attraction
  Hot Springs
Fee: $10
Facilities:
  Picnic Area
  Camping
  Lodging

Tiny Town and Railroad
6249 S Turkey Creek Rd, Tiny Town CO 80465

WEB SITE: www.tinytownrailroad.com
PHONE: 303-697-6829
COORDINATES: 39.6029 | -105.2230

> *Attraction*
> *Cable, Cog, Incline, Train Rides*
> **Fee**: $5
> **Interstate**:
>   I-70 Exit 260; 10.8 miles

DESCRIPTION: Tiny Town was created at the site of the Denver-Leadville stagecoach stop in a scenic mountain canyon southwest of Denver in 1915. That's when George Turner began constructing one-sixth-sized buildings for his young daughter. In 1920, the town was opened to the public and now contains over 100 colorful buildings. In 1939, the Tiny Town Railway began transporting adults and children through the village. **SEASON & HOURS**: Memorial Day through Labor Day, daily, 10am to 5pm. May and September, weekends, 10am to 5pm. **DIRECTIONS**: From I-70 Exit 260 go south 5.2 miles on SR-470, west 4.9 miles on US-285, and southeast .8 miles on S Turkey Creek Rd.

Tread of Pioneers Museum
800 Oak St, Steamboat Springs CO 80487

WEB SITE: www.yampavalley.info/treadofpioneers.asp
PHONE: 970-879-2214
COORDINATES: 40.4871 | -106.8339

> *Museum*
> *History - Local*
> **Fee**: $5
> **Facilities**:
>   Gift Shop

DESCRIPTION: Housed within the 1908 Victorian-style home are numerous artifacts from the ranching, mining and pioneer lifestyle of Routt County residents. Additional rooms display a History of Skiing exhibit, Native American art, an extensive collection of firearms, and a collection of historic photographs from the Routt County area. The museum also offers visitors the use of their oral history library and research library as well as a Kid's Scavenger Hunt. **SEASON & HOURS**: Year-round, Tuesday through Saturday, 11am to 5pm. **DIRECTIONS**: In town at the corner of 8th St and Oak St.

United States Mint
320 W Colfax Ave, Denver CO 80204

WEB SITE: www.usmint.gov/mint_tours/?action=StartReservation
PHONE: 303-405-4761
COORDINATES: 39.7400 | -104.9923

> *Attraction*
> *Educational*
> **Fee**: Free
> **Interstate**:
>   I-25 Exit 210A; 1.2 miles
> **Facilities**:
>   Gift Shop

DESCRIPTION: Guided tours of the United States Mint demonstrate the present state of coin manufacturing and the history of the Mint. Visitors learn about the craftsmanship required at all stages of the minting process, from the original designs and sculptures to the actual striking of the coins. Tours start on the hour; reservations are required. On-site parking is not provided; public lots and meters are nearby. **SEASON & HOURS**: Year-round, Monday thru Friday, 8am to 2pm. **DIRECTIONS**: From I-25 Exit 210A go east 1.2 miles on Colfax Ave.

Ute Indian Museum
17253 Chipeta Dr, Montrose CO 81401

WEB SITE: www.coloradohistory.org/hist_sites/uteindian/ute_indian.htm
PHONE: 970-249-3098
COORDINATES: 38.4350 | -107.8673

DESCRIPTION: Situated in the heart of the Ute territory once homesteaded by Chief Ouray, the Ute Museum contains the most complete collection of Ute relics in the nation. A number of permanent and changing exhibits give visitors a glimpse of history from the perspective of the Ute Indians, celebrating their culture. The grounds include Chief Ouray Memorial park, Chipeta's Crypt, and a garden. **SEASON & HOURS**: Year-round, Tuesday through Saturday, 9am to 4pm. **DIRECTIONS**: Located 3 miles south of town off US-550 at Chipeta Dr.

Museum
History - Local
Fee: $4
Facilities:
Visitor Center
Gift Shop
Picnic Area

White River Museum
565 Park Ave, Meeker CO 81641

WEB SITE: www.meekercolorado.com/museum.htm
PHONE: 970-878-9982
COORDINATES: 40.0385 | -107.9133

DESCRIPTION: Visitors can travel through the museum viewing women's fashion from the late 1800's to 1940's as well as the uniforms of officers in World War 1. The museum also contains artifacts unique only to Meeker, including several personal items belonging to Meeker's colorful residents of the past, most notably Nathan Meeker, the founder of Meeker, Colorado, and the man whose actions led to the Meeker Massacre. **SEASON & HOURS**: Mid-April through November, daily, 9am to 5pm. December to mid-April, daily, 10am to 4pm. **DIRECTIONS**: From I-70 Exit 90 go north 42.2 miles on SR-13 then turn left two blocks on 6th St and right at Park Ave.

Museum
History - Local
Fee: Free
Interstate:
I-70 Exit 90; 42.3 miles

The Wildlife Experience
10035 S Peoria, Parker CO 80134

WEB SITE: www.thewildlifeexperience.org
PHONE: 720-488-3300
COORDINATES: 39.5346 | -104.8447

DESCRIPTION: The Wildlife Experience presents information about the world's wildlife and ecosystems through interactive exhibits, large format film, fine art, natural history, and community educational programs. Exhibits portray the various animal species and three major ecosystems within the State: Mesas, Mountains, and Plains. The museum also features exhibits specifically designed for children 12 and under. Films are shown on a 40-by-60 foot screen every hour between 10am and 4pm in the Extreme Screen Theater. A walking trail around the museum grounds has interpretive signs that describe the grasses, trees, and wildflowers that grow along the trail. **SEASON & HOURS**: Year-round, Tuesday through Sunday, 9am to 5pm. **DIRECTIONS**: From I-25 Exit 193 go east on Lincoln Ave 1.4 miles to Peoria St and turn right .2 mile.

Museum
Animals & Nature
Fee: $10
Interstate:
I-25 Exit 193; 1.6 miles
Facilities:
Gift Shop
Food

Windsor Museum
301 Walnut St, Windsor CO 80550 (City Hall)

WEB SITE: www.ci.windsor.co.us/index.asp?NID=464
PHONE: 970-674-2400
COORDINATES: 40.4818 | -104.9058

Museum
History - Local
Fee: Free
Interstate:
I-25 Exit 262; 4.6 miles

DESCRIPTION: Visitors can explore Windsor's past as they stroll through the buildings most influential in shaping the town. The four restored buildings that comprise the museum are the restored Railroad Depot, which includes a freight room, waiting room, and station agent's room, the tiny beet shanty where several German immigrants lived, the Whitehall Schoolhouse and teacher's quarters, and the Pioneer Church. **SEASON & HOURS**: June to late August, Tuesday through Saturday, 10am to 4pm. **DIRECTIONS**: From I-25 Exit 262 go east 4.5 miles on SR-392/CR-68 then north .1 mile on 6th St.

Yampa River Botanic Park
PO Box 775088, Steamboat Springs CO 80477

WEB SITE: http://steamboatsprings.net/departments/parks_recreation/parks/botanical_park
PHONE: 970-879-4300
COORDINATES: 40.4725 | -106.8286

Nature & Wildlife
Arboretum / Garden
Fee: Free

DESCRIPTION: At the Yampa River Botanical Park, visitors will see a variety of plants, trees, and shrubs that grow at an altitude of 6,800 feet. The five-acre park has over 40 gardens; sculptures are scattered throughout the gardens. Flowering comes to peak in June and July. The park's proximity to the river attracts a variety of birds. Special events occur during summer. **SEASON & HOURS**: Open daily from dawn to dusk May through October. **DIRECTIONS**: From town center go south .8 mile on US-40/Lincoln Ave, west .1 mile on Trafalger Dr, and south .2 mile on Pamela Ln to parking lot. The park is south of the soccer fields.

Made in the USA
Coppell, TX
19 December 2019